David Hodge is an encourager. It's in his heart. It's in his blood. It's what he lives, breathes, and does. And if you read his book, not only will you be encouraged but you'll learn how to be an encourager too. It's never too late to make a legacy . . . or to change the one you're leaving.

—John Houchens, President, Sixty Feet, Kampala, Uganda

I've known David for decades and have learned a great deal from him. *Your Legacy* crystallizes his life message beautifully. I read it all in one evening but now I plan to read it again slowly to get these powerful principles off the page and into my life.

—Phil Tuttle, President & CEO,
Walk Thru the Bible Ministries, Atlanta, GA

David Hodge has written a powerful and compelling work. Read this book and learn from this authentic follower of the risen Christ.

—Colonel Kenneth W. Maynor,
Territorial Commander, The Salvation Army, Tokyo, Japan

This book is a wonderful and thought-provoking guide that could help any organization think about their legacy and encourage any team to develop a lasting legacy for their next generation of leaders.

—Bill Fischer, CEO, Evans Roofing Company, Elmira, NY

Your Legacy is a *must* for every leader, parent, teacher, and follower of Jesus Christ.

—Dr. Thomas B. Webber, CAPT, USN (Ret.),
Director of Samaritan's Purse Operation Heal Our Patriots, Boone, NC

David's book is a conversation about significant matters. You'll come away informed, inspired, and encouraged.

—Walt Wiley, President, Winning with Encouragement, Charlotte, NC

Your Legacy is the book we all need to build a legacy worth remembering.

—Jesse DeYoung, Executive Campus Pastor,
Flatirons Community Church, Lafayette, CO

Your Legacy awakened my spirit. Serving Christ through construction is the legacy we were led to embrace by David, and now we have a book that will encourage others in pursuit of their legacy.

—Bart Azzarelli, CEO, Dallas 1 Corporation, Thonotosassa, FL

This book is fun. This book is inspirational. This book is practical. This book is . . . well . . . encouraging! Just like David.

—Dr. Keith Moore, Senior Pastor, Dogwood Church, Peachtree City, GA

David Hodge has modeled a life of integrity and gives a practical but challenging way to be sure that the legacy we leave will impact people long after we are gone.

—Dr. Bill Welte, President and CEO, America's Keswick, Whiting, NJ

Legacy is a word thrown around Christian circles a lot. We speak about its importance but rarely are we shown how to leave a godly one. Until now. David Hodge not only highlights what it takes to leave a legacy, but points us to the one who is our ultimate guide, Jesus Christ.

—Roy Baldwin, Executive Director,
Monadnock Christian Ministries, Jaffrey, NH

As you read these pages, your soul will be encouraged.

—Terence Chatmon, President, EQUIP Leadership, Duluth, GA

This is not only a great read, it's a great challenge. May we all accept that challenge and choose how we live each day to truly leave a God-honoring legacy!

—Cathy Berggren, Executive Director,
The Real Life Center, Peachtree City, GA

A tremendous read, sure to inspire.

—Jan Kary, CFRE, Principal Consultant,
Jan Kary & Associates, Columbia, MD

YOUR LEGACY

Designing a Life That Honors God, Blesses Others & Brings Joy to Your Own Soul

David Hodge

Your Legacy: Designing a Life That Honors God, Blesses Others & Brings Joy to Your Own Soul

Discovery House is affiliated with Our Daily Bread Ministries, Grand Rapids, Michigan.

Requests for permission to quote from this book should be directed to: Permissions Department, Discovery House, PO Box 3566, Grand Rapids, MI 49501, or contact us by email at permissionsdept@dhp.org.

Interior design by Michael J. Williams

ISBN: 978-1-62707-953-2
Printed in the United States of America
First printing in 2019

For Pam.
My compassionate, funny, brave,
inspiring, and superhot wife.

CONTENTS

PREFACE

My mission in life—my calling and passion—is to *encourage* people.

Encouragement is important because we live in a fallen and broken world where it's easy to lose hope. We have a fierce enemy who relentlessly seeks to steal our joy and destroy our lives. Using deception and accusation, Satan is an expert at discouragement.

This ugly reality is why the Bible urges believers to "encourage one another daily" (Hebrews 3:13).

"Encourage" is a fine translation for *parakaleo*, the Greek verb used in this verse, but it can't quite capture all the verb's nuances. Its roots are *para*, meaning "beside," and *kaleo*, meaning "to call or call out." Picture that: One person coming alongside another and calling out words that need to be heard.

This is the essence of encouragement: we draw near to others and tell them what they need to hear. We shore up the shaky, inspire the weary, hearten the timid, and reassure those who doubt.

You've needed this kind of encouragement. You might even be there today. When life beats up on you and you feel like quitting, encouragement is like wind in your sails. It's a pat on the back from a trusted friend. It's like water to a thirsty plant. Although God alone knows exactly when your current trials will end, a brother or sister in Christ can always put an arm around you and tell you things like, "You *will* get through this. I know it's bleak right now, but it won't always be." With confidence in God's character and the promises of Scripture, others can gently reassure us with these comforting words because the Lord pledges to be with all His children and lead us home.

Another form of encouragement—exhortation—has a harder edge. It also stems from love and concern, but it's not exactly a pat on the back. (In fact, it's administered a bit lower on the backside, perhaps even with a foot!) It's a wake-up call. It's where others urge us to action, remind us of hard truth, or boldly call us to embrace different attitudes.

I experienced this recently after speaking for the second time to a group of leaders in a hospice ministry. Talk about a group that I respect! They hold people's hands, let them know that God loves them, and help them navigate the mystery of life's final days. After I got home, I received a fat package of handwritten cards thanking me for my ministry. This envelope full of encouragement came just as I was about to leave for another speaking engagement. Their kind and genuine words reminded me never to underestimate the power of a simple thank-you note.

As I was putting the last card back in the envelope, I noticed something. The note was addressed to "Doug." I'm ashamed to admit it, but in a very shallow sort of way, this honest mistake got underneath my skin. *Doug? Really? I just spent a whole day with these people and they can't even remember my name?*

Almost immediately the Spirit of God convicted me about my bad attitude. I had to confess, "Lord, I'm sorry. I realize it doesn't matter if anyone knows my name. I know that." And as I sat there I felt God say to me, "David, *I* know your name."

In this instance it was the Lord who came alongside me and called out words I needed to hear. They were words of comfort *and* correction. God both encouraged and exhorted me. I hope, as you read these pages, that your soul will be encouraged or exhorted—whatever is needed . . . maybe a little of both.

According to the writer of Hebrews, we don't just need an occasional pep talk. *Every day* we need people who will inspire us to keep going. And *every day* we need to come alongside others who are in need of a spiritual pick-me-up.

My prayer is twofold: first, that through this exploration of *Your Legacy*, you will be encouraged from God's Word, and second, that you will decide to encourage others daily by applying these eternal truths.

PART 1

RECEIVING A LEGACY

1

ONE DAY IN COOPERSTOWN

> Your story is the greatest legacy that you will leave to your friends. It's the longest-lasting legacy you will leave to your heirs.
>
> Steve Saint

We hear the word *legacy* all the time. A simple Google search of the word finds over a billion results in less than a second. If you browse long enough, you'll find titles like:

Mom Leaves Legacy of Love
School's Legacy Resonates a Century Later
Foul Legacy: The Children of Terrorism

Fallen Officer's Legacy Remembered a Year After His Death
The Legacy of China's One-Child Policy

But what exactly *is* a legacy? *Legacy* is generally defined as something that is passed along from an ancestor or predecessor or as a carryover from the past. Often, this is simply a passive process, the natural result of time.

For our purposes, we're going to define it this way:

A legacy is what you leave behind for others.

For most of my life I used this word mindlessly. I failed to appreciate it fully. I didn't grasp the importance of a good legacy. It took a once-in-a-lifetime trip with my brother to open my eyes.

Growing up, Kevin and I alternated between close friends and worst enemies—best explained by the fact we were only 18 months apart in age. Like most siblings, we clashed often, usually over trivial things. However, we had this in common: we were huge baseball fans. More specifically, we shared a passion for the Cincinnati Reds during the glorious "Big Red Machine" days of the 1970s. Cheering together for legendary players like Johnny Bench, Pete Rose, and Joe Morgan was one of the highlights of our childhood.

Kevin and I never imagined that we would one day visit the National Baseball Hall of Fame in Cooperstown, New York. But as adults, we made the pilgrimage together. We spent a long weekend there, and it was everything we dreamed of and more. Each day for three wonderful days we roamed those storied halls. Each evening we came back to the "Big Red Machine" exhibit and recalled magical moments from our childhood. And then it was time to go.

Just before we were due to head back to the airport, Kevin decided to pick up some last-minute souvenirs for his children. While he shopped, I sat on a bench agonizing. A store called National Pastime was selling an autographed photo of Johnny Bench. The Reds' perennial all-star catcher was my hero growing up. But this particular piece of memorabilia was expensive! Should I spend so much money? (More importantly, could I buy it without my wife, Pam, finding out?)

As I went back and forth in my mind, I was struck—out of left field, no doubt—by a profound thought. The people who had impacted me most in life weren't baseball players. The great Johnny Bench was certainly fun to watch. I was privileged to see him do amazing things with a bat, ball, and glove. But though he gave me some great sports moments, he never did anything for me personally. Sitting there I realized that the most significant people in my life were (and are) the ones who have cared for me, loved me, accepted me, and been patient with me.

My mind was made up. I walked into a store called the Cooperstown Bat Company, and I had them engrave a custom baseball bat with my name and, under that, the simple phrase, "An Influenced Life."

Eagerly, I returned home, called my mom and dad, who lived just a few miles away, and invited them to join Pam and me for breakfast the following Saturday. When the day came, I shared with them my souvenir story and my Cooperstown epiphany. I got to tell them they were the three people who had had the biggest impact in my life and that I couldn't imagine where I might be without them.

I shared first with my dad all he has meant to me. I did the same with my mother and finally with Pam. Then, taking out my customized bat, I asked them to autograph it.

Since that time, I have added a number of other signatures to my bat. Whenever God reminds me of a significant person from my past or brings someone new into my life who has a life-changing impact on me, I schedule a meeting with that person. I tell them simply, "This is what you mean to me . . ." When I'm finished, I say, "I would be honored if you would autograph my bat."

Each time I do this, and every time I look at my bat, I am reminded that what I am today is because of the people who have come alongside me and invested their lives in me.

(I especially love my mother's autograph. In parentheses, she added "Mom"—as if I might forget who she is!)

It took a trip to Cooperstown and an afternoon of souvenir shopping to remind me in a powerful way that a legacy is simply what we leave behind for others.

Looking back on those moments on the bench in upstate New York, I now realize it was the prompting of the Holy Spirit that changed my focus. It was a clear conviction to make a difference in the lives of others. The truth is, God has put a host of people in my life who have blessed me, encouraged me, and mentored me. Each has made my life better by pointing to a more excellent way. That day, the question came upon me: Am I that person to others?

QUESTIONS FOR REFLECTION

1. Oftentimes we don't think much about someone's legacy until after his or her death. Or we don't think about our own legacy until late in life. Why is this? Why is this a mistake?
2. What's the most precious *material* possession an ancestor ever handed down to you?
3. What's the best *example* someone ever left behind for you?
4. What's the best *lesson* a predecessor ever passed on to you?

5. Who has had a major impact on your life? Write down the first three people who come to mind.
6. If a legacy is simply what you leave behind for others, what are some of the things you'd be leaving behind if the Lord called you home today?
7. Before we proceed, here's the biggest question of all: Are you leaving behind what you want to leave behind?

2

EVERYONE LEAVES A LEGACY

> All happenings great and small are parables whereby God speaks; the art of life is to get the message.
>
> Malcolm Muggeridge

One morning in 1888, Alfred Nobel was eating breakfast and reading the newspaper. Imagine his shock when he began to read his own obituary! Imagine his horror when his premature death notice appeared under the grim headline, "The Merchant of Death Is Dead"!

The unflattering title, "Merchant of Death," was due to the fact that Alfred Nobel was the inventor of dynamite. He intended for his "TNT" to be used in the construction of roads and railways; however, when military planners realized its explosive power, it was promptly weaponized.

Consequently, Nobel's noble invention was responsible for the deaths of tens of thousands of soldiers on the battlefields of Europe.

The record was eventually set straight—it was actually Alfred's brother Ludwig who had died—but the misprint had far-reaching effects. Historians believe Alfred was so badly shaken by this obituary that he modified his will, earmarking the bulk of his vast estate for the funding of annual awards for noteworthy academic, cultural, and scientific achievements. Upon his death in 1896, Nobel's wishes began to be carried out—the most prestigious honor being the famous Nobel Peace Prize.

This is how Alfred Nobel is remembered today—not as "the Merchant of Death" but as a great proponent of international peace and progress. All because Nobel, upon reading his own obituary eight years prior to his passing, decided he wanted to leave a different and better legacy.

Paul J. Meyer, a pioneer in motivational leadership, once said, "Everything you are and possess today, whether good or bad, will pass down to those who come after you."

It's a powerful thought, isn't it? Not just the things you *have*, but everything you *are* will eventually be passed down to those who come after you. You will leave behind a legacy. The question is, *What will your legacy be?*

Again, let's be clear. It's not a question of *if* you are going to leave something behind. You will. We all do. The question is, *Are you going to leave behind what you really want to leave behind?*

Maybe, like Alfred Nobel, you've had a moment in your life when God shook you up and got your attention. This happened for me several years ago. Thank heaven for such wake-up calls!

I returned home from Portland, Oregon, late on a Friday when everyone else was already asleep. I woke up first thing Saturday morning because I was leaving again Sunday for another speaking engagement, and I had much to do. (I still travel a good bit in my work; in those years I was traveling far too much.)

My daughter, Elizabeth, was the first one down for breakfast. I'll never forget what happened in those next few moments.

Let me paint the scene: Elizabeth sits at the table, eating her Lucky Charms. As she eats, I'm telling her everything I want her to accomplish that day—all the things she neglected to do while I was gone plus the other things she needs to do over the weekend.

She doesn't speak, which is unusual for her, because she likes to talk—just like her dad. She doesn't make a peep until she finally lifts her head and says innocently, "Hey, Dad, why are you always so grumpy when you come back from a long trip?"

I immediately got defensive. "I'm not grumpy!" I protested grumpily. (Though inwardly I wasn't so sure.)

Later I asked my wife, Pam, "Honey, I'm not grumpy when I get back from trips, am I?" There was a long pause, before she said diplomatically, "Well, not *always*."

Malcolm Muggeridge, the legendary British journalist, once observed, "All happenings great and small are parables whereby God speaks; the art of life is to get the message."

That day I got the message. That small happening, that simple exchange with my daughter, changed my life in significant ways.

As I reflected on what God was saying to me through "The Parable of the Lucky Charms Breakfast," I realized I was giving the best of me to strangers and holding back the worst part of me for the people I treasure most in life.

At the time I was working with a ministry called Winning with Encouragement. And truly, the encouragement for which I most want to be remembered is encouraging my family.

I realized that Saturday I'd never accomplish my goal if I kept going down the path I was going. I would have to become much more intentional.

It occurred to me that whenever I go somewhere and speak, I work hard preparing for that time, because I want very much to connect with groups and see hearts changed. I want to bless the audiences I am privileged to stand in front of, so I pray, study, brainstorm, think creatively, and review and rework my messages. All this effort and intentionality for "strangers." My conscience pricked: Shouldn't I do at least that much in my role as a husband and father? I made a vow that day to do everything in my power for the rest of my days to encourage my family.

Sometimes we give our best to others and save the worst for the nearest and dearest people in our lives. What a sad and forgettable way to live! Those aren't the memories you want to pass on to your loved ones. Certainly, I don't want that for my family.

We all need hope that it is possible to reverse the course of our negative impact. During this period, I was reminded of the Old Testament story of Jacob. Jacob lived his early years as a selfish and greedy individual—especially toward his family. But in Genesis 28, we see a complete change in Jacob's attitude toward God and those closest to him. And because of that encounter with God, he began a course of action that positively impacted generations to come. Jacob's life ended with God identifying himself with this once self-centered man: "I am the God of Abraham, the God of Isaac and the God of Jacob" (Exodus 3:6).

The sobering thought is that we only have one life to make a difference. Speaker and author Beth Moore profoundly captured the urgency: "This is our time on the history line of God. This is it. What will we do with the one deep exhale of God on this earth? For we are but a vapor and we have to make it count."

We want to leave a good legacy. And we want to leave a lasting one.

Dr. James Dobson, the popular parenting expert, author, and founder of Focus on the Family, tells a story: When he was at Pasadena College (now Point Loma Nazarene University), his number one goal was to have his name on a tennis trophy. Long story short, his goal eventually became a dream come true.

Years after he graduated, Dr. Dobson received a phone call from a friend and former classmate. The message? His trophy was found in a dumpster behind one of the administrative buildings. His friend refurbished the trophy and sent it to him.

Dr. Dobson's takeaway from that experience? "If you live long enough, life will trash your trophies."

It's interesting, isn't it? The things we sometimes think are so crucial are ultimately not that important. And oftentimes the things we don't give much attention to are the very things that are going to last into eternity. It's those eternal things we want to focus on in this book.

Carl C. Wood said, "If we work our fingers to the bone, pinch and save every penny for a rainy day, who knows, before no time at all we may be the richest person in the cemetery." This happens so often in our society—people giving themselves to things that will not last.

We're after something very different. John C. Maxwell summarizes a wiser perspective: "When you're 80 years old, looking back over your life while rocking on your front porch, personal satisfaction and career goals may not seem quite as significant as they once did. What will likely be much more important is what you did with your life that was of lasting value."

We're asking that question: What does it take to leave a good legacy that truly lasts? In the next chapter, using Jesus as our model, we'll look at three things He did to leave a good and lasting legacy. Are you ready to step up to the starting line?

QUESTIONS FOR REFLECTION

1. Alfred Nobel got to read his obituary eight years early—giving him the opportunity to change his legacy. How might your obituary read today if a reporter wrongly assumed you'd died yesterday?
2. What do you think of the famous statement, "Nobody on his deathbed ever said 'I wish I had spent more time on my business'"?
3. What are the things for which you'd most like to be remembered?

3

AT THE STARTING LINE

When people are serving, life is no longer meaningless.

John W. Gardner

I ran track when I was in high school. I was a sprinter and a member of our 440-relay team. (That tells you how old I am—this was back in the day when races were still measured in *yards*.)

If you've never had the experience of running track, you may not realize the precision, strategy, and hard work that goes into the sprint relays. Staying in your lane, not dropping the baton—all of that is harder than most people think. When everything goes right, the relay is beautiful to behold. But when something goes wrong—as it did for both the American men's and women's teams in the 2008 Summer Olympics—it's neither fun to participate in nor pleasant to watch.

I mention my track career because I'm pretty sure I could have been an Olympic sprinter. Only one small thing kept me from gold medal glory: my lack of world-class speed. No, seriously, I bring up my track experience because leaving a legacy is a lot like a relay race. We receive, in a sense, a baton from the previous generation. We run the race of life. Then we pass the baton to the next generation.

As a former track guy, I can tell you that much of a team's success depends on what happens before the race—all that planning at the starting line.

As we begin this process of trying to leave a lasting legacy, what do we need to know? What practical things do we need to keep in mind? I'm convinced all great legacies begin at the starting line with three habits.

1. All great legacy builders start with a plan.

J. Otis Ledbetter writes in his book *Your Heritage*, "The chief reason many of us fail to give a solid heritage is not lack of desire, incompetence, or even baggage from the past. The number one reason we fail to give a solid heritage is negligence—we neglect to create a plan for doing so."

It's so obvious, so simple, so sobering, isn't it? Every successful venture requires planning. How much more so the eternally significant venture of leaving a legacy.

Jesus had a plan. Do you remember how He expressed it? "The Son of Man did not come to be served, but to serve, and to give his life as a ransom for many" (Mark 10:45). In other words, Jesus was crystal clear about why He was on earth and what His purpose was—He came to seek, serve, and save sinners. I believe we leave the best and most enduring legacy when we have a clear plan.

Ken Blanchard is famous for his best-selling books on leadership and management. As he travels and interacts with people, he asks this question: "Would you like to make the world a better place for having been here?"

Blanchard says he has asked that question *thousands* of times through the years. To date no one has ever said, "No." His follow-up question is this: "What is *your plan* for leaving the world a better place?" According to Blanchard, nine out of every ten people he's talked with have no answer. They stare blankly, hang their head, or fumble an answer. The truth is, they have no plan.

True confession: Until I started thinking hard about this concept of building a legacy, I had no plan either! So if you are among the 90 percent with no clear plan for making a difference in the world, don't despair. The purpose of this book is to give you the framework, show you a biblical model, and walk you through some practical steps to help you leave a good legacy. In these pages I'm going to encourage you to create a solid, workable plan. With that plan you'll be able to leave behind exactly what you want to leave behind.

If you're open to God's guidance, He can do remarkable things in your life. This is an opportunity, maybe for the first time in your life, to sit down and say, "Lord, what do you want me to leave behind? How do you want me to impact people for your kingdom? What specific steps do you want me to take?"

I'm not sure how God will answer those questions, but you can be sure that your legacy plan will not look exactly like anyone else's. Because we are all diverse and unique, it will be unique to you. If you study the people in the Bible, you will see that they were all gifted in different ways and called to different tasks. We'll look at the details of all that later. The point is, if you want to leave an enduring legacy, you're going to need a plan.

2. All great legacy builders focus on relationships.

I often get distracted by trivial things. On one particular trip to the grocery store, I saw a jar of Cheez Whiz and smiled broadly. How could I not? Just saying the words "Cheez Whiz" makes me happy. When I got home, I tried to find cheezwhiz.com on the internet. Alas, there is no such website! But at kraft.com, I learned that Cheez Whiz was invented in 1953. That's all I know. Pretty useless information, right?

Totally useless. But here's a fact that's not cheesy or trivial. In fact, you might want to highlight this statement: All of the Ten Commandments have to do with relationships. Did you know that? The first four deal with our relationship with God. The final six focus on our relationships with others.

Here's another significant truth: The Great Commandment that Jesus gave us in Luke 10:27—"'Love the Lord your God with all your heart and with all your soul and with all your strength and with all your mind'; and, 'Love your neighbor as yourself'"—is also about relationships. According to Jesus, the Great Commandment has two parts. Above all else, we are to pursue an all-consuming love relationship with God. After that—and connected to that—we are to love the people around us. Life as God intended is all about relationships of love.

Here's how Jesus modeled these two primary love relationships. He loved His Father in heaven above all else, saying, "I can do nothing on my own. . . . I carry out the will of the one who sent me, not my own will" (John 5:30 NLT).

The Greek verb translated *carry out* (or *seek* in some translations) is both active and proactive. Essentially Jesus was saying, "Every day I diligently determine to do the

Father's will." This is how He demonstrated His love for the Father—through radical trust and obedience.

Jesus also made loving others a top priority. In His own words, He "came to seek and save those who are lost" (Luke 19:10 NLT).

I love the story of William and Catherine Booth. They founded the Salvation Army in England in the mid 1860s primarily to help those addicted to alcohol. As this "army" grew and the ministry expanded into many different cultures across the world, the Booths wanted to encourage their missionaries (officers) with a message of hope and direction. One year, William sent a one-word telegram greeting to each missionary around the world. The word? *Others*. The Booths' desire was to remind the leaders of the Salvation Army why they were doing what they were doing. Their mission was fundamentally relational—to share the love of God with people in need.

William and Catherine Booth left an impressive legacy, and Jesus, of course, left the greatest legacy ever. The reason is that they had a clear plan. In both cases, the plan was to be extremely intentional about relationships. We need to do the same. Knowing that God first loved us, we reciprocate—loving Him with all that we are, then letting His love flow through us and out of us, splashing into the lives of others.

Is that happening in your life? Are you cultivating relationships in which you both experience and express the love of God? Emails, text messages, social media posts—all those things have their place. But nothing replaces face-to-face relationships and time spent together. Are you coming alongside the people God has put in your life? Are you calling out words they need to hear? Someone has wisely said, "Present your family members and friends with their eulogies now. They won't be able to hear how much you love and appreciate them from inside a coffin."

I work very hard at doing this. Like all parents, I long to connect with my children. And like most, I am continually realizing I have a lot to learn about connecting.

From my daughter, for example, I learned that with teenagers, there is that moment in a retail store when you're walking along and you suddenly realize your child is intentionally lagging three steps behind you so no one will think she is "with you." That was a devastating moment for me. I'm still dealing with it. But not every moment is so traumatic. At some point I noticed that whenever I picked Elizabeth up from school, took her to Outback, and ordered a Bloomin' Onion, she wouldn't stop talking. I found a fun way to connect with her.

I connect with my son Jameson through baseball. We go to games, do road trips, and watch baseball on TV. We even watch movies about baseball. That's how we connect.

Some time ago Pam and I were talking about my relationships with our children. "David," she said, "you need to spend some time with Spencer." Pam is one of the great encouragers in my life. She is also one of my great exhorters. Typically, she does them both together. She's very good at it (and very sneaky too).

At the time of this conversation, Spencer was only five years old—a sweet kid, but with a seemingly endless supply of energy. Pam was saying that I needed to work harder connecting with him. I knew she was right, and I made a mental note: *I need to work on connecting with Spencer.*

Not long after that, I was packing for a trip to New York for a few days. You need to understand that when I pack it's sort of like a holy experience. I like to be alone. There are so many details I need to remember. I can't afford to forget anything.

I was fully engaged in my intense packing ritual and Spencer was running in and out of the room. He was just playing and having a good time, just being a five-year-old boy, but he was really getting in my way and on my nerves. Pam sensed my frustration, so she grabbed him as he swooped by and took him downstairs. Bless her.

When I got to New York and unpacked, I found in my luggage a single Lego brick. Spencer must have dropped the Lego into my bag while I was packing.

For some reason, I went to Lego.com, and I discovered that *Lego* is Danish for "play well." It is also Latin for "I put together." That concept of "I put together" stuck with me for the next couple of days.

What do you do with a Lego? You put it with another Lego, and another, and you create some really cool things. As I was thinking through the whole concept—I'm a very visual person—I thought, *That's what I need to do with Spencer. I need to connect with him. And that's probably not going to happen if I insist on doing that on my terms only.*

When I got back from my trip, Spencer and I built gigantic walls with his preschool-sized Legos. (Bonus trivia: They're called Duplos, derived from the Latin word for "double" because they're twice the height, width, and depth of the standard bricks.) After setting them up, he would run full speed, crash into them, and knock them down. We'd set them up and he'd smash them again . . . and again . . . and again. In true Lego fashion, we "played well . . . together." We connected.

This experience reminds me that we need to look intentionally for ways to connect in love with the people around us. If we are wise, we will do it on their terms, not just ours.

3. All great legacy builders possess an attitude to serve.

Think of the attitudes people embrace (and project into the world around them). Some people are cheerful, grateful, generous, and others-centered. You can't wait to see them. Others are dour, bitter, stingy, and self-absorbed. You wish they'd go away.

We forget that attitude is a choice. Chuck Swindoll has written, "The longer I live the more convinced I become that life is 10 percent what happens to us and 90 percent how we respond to it." Every day we can choose positive, right attitudes.

I will never forget when my daughter became a teenager. Like most adolescents, she had a mouth on her. She wasn't just full of attitude, she was attitude dressed in a skirt! Yet seeing now how much she has matured, I'm reminded that our attitudes can change.

Without a doubt, the single most significant decision I can make on a daily basis is my choice of attitude. I have to make this decision early, when I first wake up. If I don't, it is already made for me. Thankfully, we don't need to look within to find our daily motivation. As Holocaust survivor Corrie ten Boom expressed it, "If there's one thing I've learned since I've passed my eightieth birthday, it's that I can't store up good feelings and behavior—but only draw them fresh from God each day."

This is the big question that looms: *Who am I here to serve?* If I don't stop to consciously ask that question, do you know whom I'll end up serving? Me! I know this from years of real-life experience.

Selfishness is the chronic issue in my relationship with God. Each day I have to wrestle with these questions: *Do I believe God exists solely to make me happy? Or do I believe I exist solely to bring Him glory?*

A self-centered attitude is also the number one challenge in my human relationships—my friendships and working relationships. It's the biggest problem in my marriage.

The question in all my relationships is, *Will I live for self or will I choose to serve God and others?* I have to *choose* to do the latter, because it's not natural for me. I assure you, I have never accidentally stumbled into selfless service. I have to choose that mind-set. I have to decide daily that I am going to serve the people around me.

Jesus embodied this servant attitude. And Paul urges us to have the mind-set of Jesus in our earthly relationships:

> Who, being in very nature God,
> did not consider equality with God something to be used to his own advantage;
> rather, he made himself nothing
> by taking the very nature of a servant,
> being made in human likeness.
>
> (Philippians 2:5–7)

In short, Jesus chose the *attitude* of a servant, which led inevitably to the *actions* of a servant. If we are going to display Christ in our lives, then we'll need to start here, with an attitude that says, "I choose to be a servant."

QUESTIONS FOR REFLECTION

1. Are you good at planning? Why or why not?
2. What are some things you're planning in your life right now? What makes for successful planning?
3. Are you more task-oriented or people-oriented? How is either a strength or weakness in planning and fulfilling a successful legacy?
4. What relationships in your life do you most cherish and why?
5. When you read or think about *servanthood,* what five words come to mind?

4

RECEIVING THE BATON

No matter what accomplishments you make, somebody helped you.

Althea Gibson

Leaving a good legacy in life is like passing the baton in a relay race. It's not the easiest thing in the world to do.

Glancing backward, you begin running forward, being careful not to drift out of your lane. As you pick up speed, you extend your hand behind you, palm up in order to receive the baton from a teammate who is sprinting toward you. The two of you have only 20 meters (just a little over two seconds) in which to make the exchange.

That's a lot of fast-moving parts and a lot of pressure. Not surprisingly, it's easy to mess up the handoff. As a person who ran track, I remember the first time I ever saw a baton dropped in competition. Sadly, I had a close-up view of that experience, because it was *my fault*! The consequences were harsh both for our team (we were disqualified) and for me personally (the coach replaced me on the relay team in the next meet).

It was a blow, of course. But nothing compares to failing to pass on a positive, enduring legacy in life. How do we avoid fumbles and stumbles in our attempts to leave blessings to those who run after us?

A legacy is what is left behind for others. The legacy that some of us receive is profitable and precious, whether that's a godly example, unforgettable words of affirmation, wonderful memories, or intentional equipping. For others, what is received is damaging and painful, like a godless example, hurtful words, unpleasant memories, or a lifetime of neglect. For most people, it is some combination of positives and negatives.

Of great importance is how we receive the mixed bag of blessings and curses, gifts and wounds. In truth, how we receive that which is passed on by those *before* us can determine whether we will leave a positive or destructive legacy to those *after* us.

There are two traits we'll need if we want to be part of a good legacy handoff—forgiveness and gratitude. Both involve looking back.

1. We need to receive the baton with forgiveness.

Everyone (even those with good parents and positive role models) has been wounded by someone they were close to. Some of those hurts were minor and others were grave. But looking back over our lives, we all can remember times when we were damaged by people near to us or betrayed by those dear to us.

About twenty years ago I found myself in the midst of a deep depression. This wasn't the blahs or the blues; it was the kind of depression where you don't want to wake up in the morning, you don't want to see anybody, you don't want to talk with anybody. My depression was severe.

Thankfully, I connected with my pastor. Jim had an enormous influence on my life through that period. He helped me immensely.

One of the things he did as we explored my downcast heart was to encourage me to serve others. Gently but relentlessly, he kept pushing me. "David," he would say, "what you're doing right now is focusing solely on yourself." He was right. I needed to serve. I didn't necessarily *feel* like serving others, but Jim spurred me on to do that, and it was helpful.

Something else came up as Jim and I talked. One day I brought up the painful, dark truth that in my childhood I had been sexually abused. It was a painful secret deeply buried for a long time. Jim listened with grace and encouraged me with God's beautiful truth. He challenged me to take my painful situation to my Father in heaven. And he exhorted me to forgive my offender.

Jim well understood the wisdom expressed by Paul J. Meyer: "The price of forgiveness is always less than the price of unforgiveness." Jim was trying to help me grasp the piercing beauty of what author and theologian Lewis Smedes discovered: "When we forgive, we set a prisoner free and then discover that the prisoner we set free was us."

I wrestled long and hard with Jim's challenge to forgive. I remember thinking, *There's no way I can do that!*

It was on my commute to work one day that I had a breakthrough. I was listening to a cassette tape (remember those?) a friend had made for me. It was a mixtape (the older generation's version of Spotify playlists) that contained a hodgepodge of songs.

One song, titled "The Heart of the Matter," was by Don Henley (of Eagles fame). I'd never heard it before. A song of lost love, the "heart of the matter" turns out to be the need for forgiveness. And God spoke to me in those moments during rush-hour traffic. He used the words of a secular rocker to help me see that forgiveness really is the heart of the matter. I saw in a new way that my own impact in the lives of others hinged on whether or not I would let go of something that happened in my childhood.

My daughter was two years old at the time, and I remember thinking I wanted her to have a dad in her life who could trust God with pain and the desire for justice. I wanted to teach her what it truly means to forgive those who hurt you. And so I began that process.

Some time later, I was standing in a parking lot talking with another friend about forgiveness. He had been let go from a ministry several years prior. He stated, "David, I still can't forgive ____" (he named the individual who had fired him).

This friend asked if I had any counsel. I replied, "Yes, I do, because I faced a different but also painful situation. When you get up every morning say this, 'Lord, help me to forgive _____.' Say the offender's name. 'Lord, help me to forgive ______ because I can't do it on my own.'"

I reminded my friend of the story Jesus told about the widow who pestered a judge until he finally granted her request. Basically, in that passage, Jesus is telling us to pester God. To bug Him. So that's what I did. Every morning for two months I got up and said, "Lord, help me forgive _____ because I can't do it on my own."

What is amazing is that the moment I woke up and prayed that, I knew it had been done. First John 5 tells us that when we pray for things that we know are God's will, we can have absolute assurance that God will hear and grant our requests. Since God commands us to forgive (rather than suggests that we do it), we know forgiving others is His will. And we know that any time God tells His people to do something, He stands by with the grace and power we need to do it. We need to believe God can and will help us to do what seems impossible.

I said to my friend, "Try it. Every morning when you first wake up, pray, 'Lord, help me to forgive _____ because I can't do it on my own.'"

Important, life-altering matters hang in the balance. Our impact on the next generation is at stake. And peace and joy are at stake. I can tell you from experience there is more peace in forgiveness than unforgiveness. Anger and bitterness might feel good in the short-term, but they are not the route to true joy. Let me encourage you, if there's somebody you need to forgive, get before your Creator and spend time with Him, simply asking, "Lord, help me to do this. I can't do this on my own."

Since forgiveness brings freedom and bitterness is dangerous, let me ask a couple of intrusive questions: Are you holding on to a painful memory that is threatening your chances of leaving an enduring legacy? Whom do you need to forgive—especially from your formative years? A parent? A sibling? Teacher? Coach? Friend? Nothing is more important in beginning the process of leaving a positive legacy than learning to forgive those who have harmed you.

2. We need to receive the baton with gratitude.

Gratitude is a state of thankful appreciation. It might be for a kindness done or a benefit received. It might be for a comfort supplied or a discomfort eased.

Professor and psychologist Michael McCullough has innovated experimental approaches to studying gratitude. He has concluded, "Grateful people are happier, more optimistic, more satisfied with their lives. They are more empathetic toward others." That's the benefit of gratitude.

Another psychology professor, Dan McAdams, studied the willingness of adults to help younger generations. He had this to say about his study findings: "Many people say the reason they are trying to make important contributions to the future is they are grateful for blessings they received growing up."

The more we study this habit of gratitude, the more we see its tremendous ripple effects.

Of course, we shouldn't be surprised when secular researchers champion the importance of gratitude. The Bible is filled with encouragements for us to be grateful. In the Old Testament, we read, "Give thanks to the LORD, for he is good! His faithful love endures forever" (Psalm 118:1 NLT). The New Testament gives this exhortation from the apostle Paul: "Be thankful in all circumstances, for this is God's will for you who belong to Christ Jesus" (1 Thessalonians 5:18 NLT). God's will. If we take that to its logical conclusion, then if we are not thankful, then we are out of God's will, a place we don't want to be.

We will never leave the legacy that God wants us to leave until we cultivate the quality of gratitude.

What are you grateful for?

The legacy Jesus gave you

The legacy Jesus gave us is the breathtaking promise of new, eternal life in Him. In light of Christ's love and grace, we have so much to be grateful for.

The apostle Paul wrote a thank-you note that we can use as a model: "I thank Christ Jesus our Lord, who has strengthened me, because He considered me faithful, putting me into service, even though I was formerly a blasphemer and a persecutor and a violent aggressor. Yet I was shown mercy . . . and the grace of our Lord was more than abundant, with the faith and love which are found in Christ Jesus" (1 Timothy 1:12–14 NASB).

Before Paul met Jesus, he was a devout Jew who was violently persecuting the church of Jesus. On his way to Damascus to imprison more Christ-followers, he had an unexpected, extremely dramatic encounter with the risen Christ. Paul was blinded, knocked flat on his back, and shaken to his core. In those moments, he likely feared for his life. He surely never thought Jesus could or would use someone like him.

True, it would be about eleven years before He began to use Paul in all the world-changing ways that we know from Scripture. But notice what Paul says to Jesus here: *You knew my past. But still you counted me faithful. You watched me, Lord, and you gave me opportunities to serve you by sharing your love with others all over the world. You showed me mercy and gave me grace, more than I deserved or imagined possible.*

Take a few minutes to write your own heartfelt letter of thanks to Jesus. Thank Him for your priceless spiritual legacy. Specifically mention the blessings that have impacted your heart the most.

The legacy others gave you

Althea Gibson was the first African-American tennis Grand Slam champion. She endured many obstacles along the way, yet she became a model of hope to many around the world. She once said, "No matter what accomplishments you make, somebody helped you." She recognized the people who helped her along the way. We all need to do that.

You are here today because at some point people took an interest in you. Maybe like me, you had parents who were tremendous role models. Maybe you came to know the Lord because your neighbors not only told you about Jesus but also showed the love of Christ in the way they lived their lives. Maybe you were impacted positively by a teacher, a youth pastor, a mentor at work, or a caring friend. There is not a person reading this sentence who has not been impacted positively by *someone*.

Remember the definition of *encourage*? It means to come alongside someone and tell them what they need to hear.

In 1992, at the summer Olympic Games, Derek Redmond, a sprinter from Great Britain, was a favorite to win a medal. Perhaps you have seen his story on TV or YouTube.

Midway through the 400-meter semifinal, Derek grabbed his right hamstring and came to an abrupt halt. Two things were instantly clear. One, he was in enormous pain, and two, his Olympic hopes were dashed. He crouched on one knee for several seconds. Then, suddenly, he stood.

Grimacing and weeping, he began hopping on one leg, determined to finish this race. As he hobbled toward the finish line, a heavyset man appeared at his side. It was Derek's brokenhearted father, who said, "You don't have to do this." Derek replied, "Yes, I do, Dad." "Well then," his father said, "we're going to do it together."

For the next 20 or 30 seconds, a worldwide audience was treated to a beautiful scene of a loving father holding up his distraught son and helping him stumble across the finish line.

Derek said later, "Hey, I realize I finished last, but, listen, I finished the race."

What a beautiful picture of the truth that we have a heavenly Father who holds us up and sees us to the finish line. What a great reminder that we have loved ones who come alongside us at critical points in life and offer help and support. And what a challenge for us to do this for others.

I attended a private Christian college. A few years ago, I went to the funeral of a professor who was very dear to me. As I was sitting at his funeral and listening to various people talk about how he had impacted their lives, my mind was filled with assorted memories of how he had impacted my life. He had kept up with my career over the years.

Every once in a while he would call me to talk and catch up. Or if I ran into him, he would tell me how proud he was of me. He was a very sweet man. He was one of those unique individuals—enormously smart yet incredibly humble. You rarely get that combination in a college professor, but that's the way he was.

What saddened me as I sat listening to the assorted eulogies is this: I never properly thanked him for his significant impact on me. Don't get me wrong . . . over the years, I occasionally expressed appreciation for this gesture or that. But I never really thanked him from my heart. I never expressed to him all the things I was thinking at his funeral.

Another of my college professors was there at the funeral. I remember looking at him, noticing for the first time how frail he was getting. I made a vow to God that I would write him a note and let him know what an enormous impact he'd had on me. His life and influence shaped me in a lot of positive ways.

When I got home, I wrote him a note and mailed it to him. About six months later I saw him and his wife, and his wife pulled me aside and said, "David, thank you for sending that letter." She paused. "He reads it every day."

What a reminder of the power of encouragement! I'm ashamed to admit that I don't express gratitude enough to those who've impacted my life. When I take the time to ponder it, I'm overwhelmed with the thought that God has filled my life with women and men whose help molded and supported me.

I believe God is honored when we display gratitude, and that He blesses a life of gratitude. Legacy builders are grateful people.

Take a few minutes right now to write a message of thanks to someone in your life who has given you a special legacy. A handwritten note will give your words added emphasis, but the important thing is that you send the message, whether that's via snail mail or email. Try to be very specific about the qualities, words, acts of kindness, and so on that this person passed on to you.

Remember, when you send a heartfelt letter of appreciation to someone, you never know how it can affect them. While you're showing appreciation of how they came alongside you when you needed it, it's also a way of coming alongside them, encouraging, supporting, and offering strength and hope.

Can you think of a better, more important practice to cultivate?

QUESTIONS FOR REFLECTION

1. What would you tell a friend who expressed great difficulty in forgiving the grievous actions of someone from his or her past? When is counseling a wise course of action?
2. What's the hardest thing you've ever had to forgive?

3. Are you a grateful person? Whatever your answer, why do you think so?
4. What are the things that keep you from expressing gratitude?

PART 2

OBSERVING A LEGACY

5

THE FOUNDATION OF A LASTING LEGACY

> It is frightening to think that we could run life's course in vain, ending up without a single work that will live on beyond the grave.
>
> Ken Boa

The legacy I most want to leave is a legacy of encouraging others.

My role model in this pursuit is a man known as Barnabas. Though he lived some two thousand years ago, his story resonates with me deeply. We meet him in the book of Acts, in a passage that describes life in the early church in Jerusalem:

> All the believers were united in heart and mind. And they felt that what they owned was not their own, so they shared everything they had. The apostles testified powerfully to the resurrection of the Lord Jesus, and God's great blessing was upon them all. There were no needy people among them, because those who owned land or houses would sell them and bring the money to the apostles to give to those in need. For instance, there was Joseph, the one the apostles nicknamed Barnabas (which means "Son of Encouragement"). He was from the tribe of Levi and came from the island of Cyprus. He sold a field he owned and brought the money to the apostles. (Acts 4:32–37 NLT)

We learn in this paragraph that Barnabas wasn't the name on this man's birth certificate—it was a nickname. Called Joseph by his parents, this Cyprian follower of Jesus was given the nickname Barnabas because of a particular quality in his life.

When I played Little League baseball, I had a good friend we called Rusty. Why do you think we called him Rusty? That's right, he was left-handed. (He also had red hair.) We gave him a nickname based on a physical attribute.

That's how nicknames come about: Often (and not always kindly) we pick out an obvious personality trait, quality, or physical attribute of a friend or colleague and bestow them with a new name—Shorty, Bucky, Ace, Doc. My wife refers to me as "stud muffin," for example. (I don't know why friends always laugh when I tell them that.)

I once read a book called *The Teammates*, which was based on four members of the Boston Red Sox during the 1940s. Johnny Pesky was one of players highlighted in the book. Pesky was not his real last name—his last name was actually Paveskovich. Apparently when Paveskovich was in the minor leagues, the sportswriters in Portland could not fit his entire name in the box score, so they shortened it to Pesky. This new name was appropriate since he was a pesky player, the kind of hitter who would get on base, bug the pitcher, steal bases, and score runs. The sportswriters referred to Johnny Paveskovich as "Johnny Pesky." The nickname stuck for the rest of his life, and later he had it legally changed.

In this description of the early church, we learn that Barnabas's real name was Joseph. But when the apostles saw his startling generosity, they said, "No way we're calling you 'Joseph'! You're not a 'Joseph' . . . you're a 'Barnabas.'" They chose this nickname because they were looking at a man who embodied what it means to encourage others.

This nickname raises a few questions: If Barnabas means *Son* of Encouragement, who is the *Father* of Encouragement?

It's God, of course. God is the source of every good and perfect thing. Isn't it true that when we have nothing, God faithfully comes alongside to meet our needs? And doesn't God give lavishly to us? In myriad ways, God constantly encourages the weak and worried, the helpless and hopeless.

Through his generous, sacrificial giving, Barnabas was reflecting God's very nature.

Don't forget the historical backdrop of Acts 4. The church had exploded into existence, and many in the prevailing Jewish culture were less than thrilled. For followers of Jesus, it was a scary and tumultuous time. Many new believers were abandoned by their Jewish friends and neighbors. Some lost their jobs. Others found their businesses boycotted.

Remember too that in Israel at this time there was no such thing as social security. There were no government welfare programs. If you found yourself in financial trouble, you turned to your family for help. Yet many who had declared allegiance to Jesus had been disowned by their families!

Barnabas arrived in Jerusalem and saw large numbers of his new sisters and brothers in Christ in serious financial need. He remembered his valuable property and realized those resources could be sold to meet the need. Notice his attitude wasn't, "This property is *mine*." In effect, Barnabas took his savings, his 401(k), and his children's inheritance (if he had kids) and sold it.

It's easy to read a passage like this and miss the significance of what Barnabas did. He took something that was very valuable and gave it away. Why? Because when God stirs compassion in your heart, you can do nothing less. Barnabas was clearly not the only generous believer in the early church, but he's one whose name we know.

This incident is one reason Barnabas is my hero and role model when it comes to the whole topic of encouragement.

In this second part of *Your Legacy*, I'd like to briefly point out six different traits I've observed while studying the lives of people who have made a positive mark on the world. These qualities explain not only *why* someone like Barnabas was able to leave such a legacy of encouragement, but *how* we too can leave enduring legacies.

Using the example of Barnabas, and the stories of other influential people of history, over the next three chapters we'll talk about six different traits that ensure a firm foundation as you run the relay to pass on a lasting legacy.

QUESTIONS FOR REFLECTION:

1. Did you have any nicknames as a kid?
2. What person from the past is a role model or hero for you? What about Bible characters . . . do you have a favorite?
3. Can you think of a time when someone has encouraged you personally through his or her generosity?
4. Why is running, whether for competition or exercise, a good metaphor for the spiritual life? What life lessons do you see in this activity?

6

WHERE IT BEGINS

> Love leaves a legacy. How you treated other people, not your wealth or accomplishments, is the most enduring impact you can leave on earth.
>
> Rick Warren

Let's go back to the relay race analogy we've been using. Here's something I know: *firm footing is critical to running a good race.*

In my heyday, my teammates and I ran on a variety of tracks that were less than ideal. Some were made of fine gravel. Others were composed of cinders. My preference was asphalt because at least it was consistent and level—most of the time, anyway. (What a shame I didn't get to run on fancy, modern, all-weather, spongy, synthetic, polyurethane track surfaces. If I'd only had that advantage . . . *and* blazing speed . . . and if the United States hadn't boycotted the 1980 Summer Olympics . . . I know in my heart I would have won *at least* two gold medals. But I digress.)

You need to know the course conditions so that you can make sure your footing is solid and secure. Otherwise, in the blink of an eye, you can find yourself flat on your back staring up at the sky. This same principle (and danger of falling) applies to our attempts to leave an enduring legacy.

Having spent countless hours analyzing the lives of those who have left a positive mark on the world, I want to point out six foundational qualities they all have in common.

The first is the beginning point of all good legacies. A positive and lasting legacy is always . . .

Motivated by Love

Love is easy to talk about and hard to comprehensively define. It has been defined as "a deep, tender, indescribable feeling of affection and concern toward a person." I love the word *indescribable*. That's what God's love is, isn't it?

But love isn't strictly emotion. As John Haggai has observed, "Love is an act of the will. . . . True love involves the totality of one's being. God, and only He, expresses it perfectly."

How does God express His love toward us? The answer is found in the very familiar words of Jesus: "For God so loved the world that he gave his one and only Son . . ." (John 3:16). He loved you and me so much that He gave the most precious gift ever. Giving is the natural instinct or outflow of love, isn't it? Love is what compels us to take what is most meaningful to us and give it to someone else.

One imperative I recognize for all who follow Jesus is our need—daily, continuously even—to return to God's love. Divine love is our salvation, our foundation, our hope, our life. The apostle Paul prayed for believers to be rooted and grounded in the Lord's love (see Ephesians 3:17–19). The apostle John reminded believers that we are able to love only because God first loved us (see 1 John 4:19).

This is true of me, and I suspect it's probably true of you as well: God's love is easy to lose sight of. We get so busy doing life, serving others, and taking care of our families and friends that we often forget the ultimate source of love. Why do I put up with fickle neighbors and moody coworkers? Why do I forgive my spouse or help my ungrateful kids? I do it all because God does all that for me. I love because He loved me enough to stir in my heart a long time ago (and He's stirring in my heart right now, if I'll only pay attention).

The infinite love of God can fill us, transform us, and flow through us to others. This is why we need to focus every day on tapping into the inexhaustible supply of God's love. When we do, we have the power to influence others immeasurably.

A few years ago, Hall of Fame basketball player Charles Barkley caused quite a stir by saying in a Nike commercial that he was *not* a role model for kids. "I am not a role model. I'm not paid to be a role model. . . . Just because I dunk a basketball doesn't mean I should raise your kids." His blunt and provocative comments sparked a heated cultural conversation.

One of the points the commercial was trying to make was valid: parents, not celebrities, should be the most important role models for their children. But in reality, kids do view the rich, famous, and successful as role models.

Fellow professional basketball player Karl Malone joined the conversation: "We don't choose to be role models, we are chosen. Our only choice is whether to be a good role model or a bad one. I love being a role model, and I try to be a positive one."

That's the better attitude. It's that kind of loving concern for others that is the attitude of a legacy builder. Barnabas was filled with that kind of love and compassion for people. He noticed when others were in trouble. He was moved with feelings of concern. But he didn't stop with emotion. Love is an act of the will. Love is a verb. It rolls up its sleeves and gets involved. Barnabas took action by selling off some of his personal assets and giving sacrificially. His generosity is reminiscent of the greatest Love ever.

This is the motivation we need if we are going to build a solid legacy. Our attitudes and actions must be rooted in the love of God.

Surely, one of the great legacies from the twentieth century belongs to Mother Teresa. All who knew about her work among the poor and dying of Calcutta, India, were struck by her loving care for those whom society had forgotten. This tiny, unassuming nun inspired thousands of people all over the world to have compassion for those with overwhelming needs. It was obvious to anyone who came in contact with her that she was motivated by love. Perhaps no better quote describes her motivation than this: "The work is the fruit of my love and my love is expressed in my work." Her zeal and works of mercy seemed to know no bounds.

In 1979, Mother Teresa was awarded the Nobel Peace Prize. By 1997, Mother Teresa's Missionaries of Charity numbered nearly 4,000 members with 610 foundations in 123 countries. All of this was accomplished because she truly cared for people. She once said, "At the end of our lives, we will not be judged by how many degrees we have acquired, how much money we have earned or how many great things we have accomplished—we will be judged by how much we loved."

What an amazing legacy of love!

Love is the beginning point of a lasting legacy, but it's not the only one. There are other qualities that sustain your efforts to make an eternal difference. A second trait that we see in the lives of influential historical characters is that they are . . .

Guided by Passion

When people are asked whom they most admire and why, one trait seems to jump out. It's *passion*. We are fascinated (and impacted most) by individuals who are passionate about certain causes or interests. Show me someone who is laser-focused on doing something with excellence, and nine times out of ten it will be a person who ends up wielding great influence.

Passion can be defined in many ways. The kind of passion we are talking about is "boundless enthusiasm." Dr. Martin Luther King Jr. declared, "If a man hasn't found something he will die for, he isn't fit to live." Before him, Ralph Waldo Emerson observed, "Nothing great was ever achieved without enthusiasm." That's a profound statement, especially when you consider what the word *enthusiasm* means. It comes from two Greek words, *en* and *theos*, which literally means "in God."

How about that? The living, loving Creator *in* you! To be *enthusiastic* from a biblical perspective means letting God breathe His life through you. Using that definition of *enthusiasm*, Emerson's statement is undeniably true. Nothing great on this earth was ever or will ever be accomplished without God Almighty breathing His life through a willing person and touching the lives of others.

In short, an enduring legacy is rooted in love, and it is guided by a holy passion. God lays on each of His children's hearts a deep, unique desire to make an eternal difference.

The movie *Chariots of Fire* is the story of Eric Liddell, an Olympic sprinter from Scotland in the mid-1920s. Liddell felt the clear calling of God to do missionary work in China. But he was also passionate about his sport. When his sister Jenny and others dismissed his athletic pursuits as trivial, Liddell delivered this now-classic response: "I believe God made me for a purpose, for China. But He also made me fast. And when I run I feel His pleasure. To give it up would be to hold Him in contempt."

Don't you love that? When you do the things God created you to do, you experience a holy pleasure. God is honored, others are blessed, and you find a deep fulfillment in your own soul. But when we do things apart from a holy passion, we hold God in contempt.

Harriet Tubman's entire life was guided by a passion to help those who were being mistreated by others. Born as a slave in 1820, she is best known for her work in the Underground Railroad, where she personally led more than three hundred slaves to freedom. She later earned the nickname "Moses" for her tireless and courageous work in providing safe passage for slaves prior to the Civil War.

But that is only part of her story. *During* the Civil War she served as a soldier, a spy, and a nurse. *After* the war she worked to ensure the rights of women. Later, she opened a home for the aged and indigent in Auburn, New York, where she continued her passionate pursuit of helping others until her death in 1913.

What's most encouraging about Harriet Tubman's story is that she was an ordinary person with a seemingly hopeless future. She was born into this world without any advantages. In fact, she was a poor slave with no rights. She had no resources—other than her extraordinary passion to serve others. It was because of that passion that she left a good and lasting legacy for many generations.

My friend Sarah Bentley is a modern example of someone with a singular passion that will have a lasting ripple effect. Her deep concern is encouraging officers in the Salvation Army. Several years ago, she recognized young officers needed help adjusting to the challenges of their first years as lieutenants. She would often share with me her thoughts on addressing the needs. Officers in the Salvation Army focus on both pastoring and addressing the most significant of human needs—a calling that can be overwhelming even for experienced officers. She worked tirelessly to create monthly mentoring groups so they could find practical help and meaningful ongoing support. Today, her dream of helping and encouraging these leaders is a reality that impacts dozens of officers every year, who in turn touch thousands of lives.

The boundless enthusiasm we call "passion" will last for generations if it's directed toward making the lives of others better. This is not a theory but a time-tested fact. It's illustrated in the lives of real people like Barnabas, Eric Liddell, Harriet Tubman, and Sarah Bentley. It can also be evident in your life.

Do you feel God's pleasure in the things you're doing? Or has your life become mainly duty and drudgery—with little true delight? To help renew your enthusiasm, your in-Godness, spend some time meditating on the love of God. Carefully, prayerfully read Romans 8, Psalm 103, or Ephesians 1. When I reflect on how precious I am to God, I find renewed passion welling up within me.

The act of building a lasting legacy must be fueled by passion. And our passions are almost always tied to our interests and abilities. Isn't it true that we tend to put our best time and energy into the things we care about and are good at? When our interests align with our talents, when our abilities begin to help meet real needs, we feel energized. Oftentimes, that's when we're knocking on the door of our legacy.

The way I express my passion will be different from the way you express your passion because our souls, personalities, and experiences are unique. Passion isn't always visible and obvious.

I once heard a story from a pastor about an experience he had at a large church in southern California. One day, while making his regular hospital visits, he found himself in the room of a church member who was deathly ill. He didn't know the woman, but in the course of their visit she said, "Pastor, I know I'm dying. And I know I have a relationship with God. I'm at peace with that. But I have a question for you: Who is going to replace me?"

The pastor got quiet when it dawned on him who this woman was. Though he didn't know her name, he recognized her as the parishioner who sat up front each Sunday and slept through his sermons. When she asked who was going to replace her, his initial thought was, "You mean who am I going to get to fall asleep on the second row every week?" Of course, he didn't say that. Instead, he asked her to explain her question.

"I get up early every Sunday morning and pray for you." Immediately, the pastor felt the deep conviction of God. The reason this woman seemed so disinterested during his sermons each week was because she was passionate about others being impacted by the preaching of God's Word! We can be so wrong about the passions of others. The reminder is this: Instead of focusing on what others are or are not doing, it's far wiser to concentrate on your own life.

An enduring legacy is motivated by love and guided by passion.

QUESTIONS FOR REFLECTION

1. Who's the most loving person you know? What does he or she do specifically to show love to others?
2. What would you tell a friend who confessed, "Right now, I just don't sense God's love, and I don't feel much compassion for others"?
3. What are your great passions? How is God stirring your heart? In what area of life is He creating enthusiasm in you?
4. What might happen if the great love of God began to guide your passions?

7

HOW IT HAPPENS

> The place God calls you to is the place where your deep gladness and the world's deep hunger meet.
>
> Frederick Buechner

The people who make the biggest difference in the world are the people who are motivated by love and guided by enthusiasm. But great legacy builders display other worthwhile traits too. For example, they are . . .

Focused by Intention

Intention is nothing more than an aim or objective that guides action.

Imagine a woman with a compass and a map, and she's in a sailboat with a rudder. Now think of another woman asleep on a raft, adrift in the middle of the sea. The first woman is focused, proactively charting a course to a precise destination. The second woman is headed wherever the wind and waves take her.

The difference between the two is like night and day. Like a zoom lens on a camera, intentionality enables us to look beyond things which are secondary or even trivial to those things that matter above all else. Intentionality, then, isn't just nice to have; it's necessary. Legacy builders don't drift into a life of impact. They are always purposeful about helping others and intentional about benefitting others.

We talked in chapter 3 about Jesus's clear plan—to seek, serve, and save the lost. He was guided by a carefully clarified objective: "to do the will of him who sent me and to finish his work" (John 4:34). That was His path—to do the will of the Father. Nothing random or haphazard.

With such crystal clear intentions, Jesus is a model for us, the very embodiment of intentionality. And His life demonstrates how big, surprising, and even amazing things happen when we have a clear objective in front of us.

Other influential people in history have singled out the importance of intentionality. J. C. Penney, the famous retail pioneer, said, "Give me a stock clerk with a goal, and I'll give you a man who will make history. Give me a man with no goals, and I'll give you a stock clerk."

For better or worse, intentionality has the power to impact people on deeper levels. Our friend Cathy leads a ministry in our community that serves individuals and families in significant financial need. Research shows that most individuals in need seek assistance again after three months, and Cathy wanted to change that. Her intention—and that of her board—was to address more than just the immediate crisis. Cathy's goal was to equip individuals and families with spiritual support and life skills that would serve them long after the most pressing physical needs were addressed. In other words, a more holistic approach. Today thousands of people in our community are better equipped because of this focused intention—and in turn, many of them are helping others.

If you're reading this sentence, God's not finished with you. You still have an opportunity to impact others. So let me ask again the question I invited you to think about at the end of chapter 2. How do you want to be remembered? No other question gets to the heart of intentionality so effectively. Wrestling with this question is immensely helpful in clarifying our own aims and objectives.

Depending on your stage of life, you may also be in a position to ask similar questions of your children, grandchildren, and other young people God puts in your path:

How do you want to be remembered? Why do you think God put you on this earth? Given your abilities and passions, your experiences and personality, what do you think might be God's specific purpose for you? Maybe that will be part of your own legacy—getting members of the younger generation to settle these crucial matters in their hearts before they go too far down the road of life. But as we'll see in the next section, that will involve more than just asking the questions.

Clear intentions are vital. They focus us on what matters. But good intentions are not enough. We will stumble in the matter of trying to leave a lasting legacy if our good intentions are not . . .

Reinforced by Action

This is so obvious that it almost seems unnecessary to mention it. Yet many intended legacies never become reality because hopes and dreams never meet with organized activity.

Henry Ford may have said it best: "You cannot build a reputation on what you are going to do."

How many times have you been frustrated by people who say they're going to do something, but then never do it? How often are you guilty of big talk followed by little action?

James 1:22 makes it clear that God doesn't want us to just be *hearers* of His Word, He wants us to be *doers* of His Word. We have to act. Otherwise, we're just deceiving ourselves. Notice Jesus didn't just talk about being a servant—He served. By his actions, Jesus *was* a servant.

A good legacy is more than words and wishes and noble thoughts. It requires effort. The good intentions of our heads and hearts must be carried out by our hands and feet. Poet Maya Angelou admonished, "Nothing will work unless you do."

For us to say we want to accomplish certain things and then make no effort toward those goals is foolish dreaming at best and hypocrisy at worst. We've all seen parents who tell their kids what is best for them—but then don't follow those principles themselves. (Hopefully we don't see such parents when we look in the mirror.) Failing to "walk the talk" leaves a legacy of disillusionment. It is the curse of do-nothingism.

As author Joel Barker said, "Vision without action is merely a dream. Action without vision just passes the time. Vision with action can change the world."

Let's review what we've seen so far. Great legacies are:

- motivated by *love*,
- guided by *passion*,
- focused by *intention*,
- reinforced by *action*, and . . .

Confirmed by Sacrifice

If you want to leave a lasting legacy, you will have to pay a personal price. Sacrifice is the yielding of something meaningful to you for the sake of someone else.

This is exactly what God did for us. "For God so loved the world that he gave his one and only Son" (John 3:16). Sacrificing your child for the sake of somebody else? Who does such a thing? Our God does. Our Father in heaven yielded something infinitely meaningful to himself.

Leaving a good and lasting legacy will not likely cost you a child, but it will surely require you to sacrifice some things of value. What is most precious to you? Time? Energy? Possessions? Hobbies? All of those are precious commodities. However, I'm learning that in this world, it's not what we take but what we give that makes us rich.

I've traveled to Cuba on nine different occasions. I love this nation, and ministering in Cuba has really opened my eyes to all the things US residents take for granted. It has changed my perspective. Showering this morning, I was reminded that in Cuba, I *never* had hot water.

On one of my Cuba trips, I was traveling with Sid, a great encourager. Whenever I am with him, I feel like a better person. (I should pay him to be my friend, now that I think about it.) Sid's a good man and a gifted evangelist. He goes to developing world countries to establish churches.

Because of the Holy Spirit working in and through Sid, dozens of house churches have been established throughout Cuba, where for many years the government would not allow new church buildings. A pastor and his family live in a couple rooms of a small house, and the rest of the structure is where the church gathers, sometimes multiple times a week.

One of the house-church pastors I met on one of my visits, Ernesto, lives and ministers in an extremely impoverished part of Cuba, several hours from Havana. Many of these Cuban believers have only the clothes on their backs, and many of them share a Bible with several other members of their house church because they don't have access to their own copy of the Scriptures.

And yet, they are amazingly generous. They give of their possessions, their time, and their lives so willingly and sacrificially. Ernesto, for example, travels miles daily—usually by foot—in order to train young pastors. Because he's been a Christian longer than anyone else in the area, in addition to all his regular pastoral duties, he takes up-and-coming leaders under his wing and disciples them.

Because of this, Sid and a doctor friend from Atlanta decided they wanted to bless Ernesto. They gave him a large sum of money and told him to purchase a motorcycle to aid in his ministry training efforts.

This humble pastor, living in such a grim section of such a desperate country was—as you might expect—overjoyed.

On a later trip, Sid and I went to meet with Ernesto to hear an update on his ministry. Talking through an interpreter, Sid asked about his motorcycle. When the interpreter translated Sid's question, Ernesto began kicking nervously at the ground and mumbling in Spanish. "I apologize, Sid," the translator relayed. "I hope this won't make you upset, but I didn't feel right using that money to buy myself a motorcycle while all the other house pastors have to walk. I hope it's okay with you, but I used your money to get us all bicycles."

Sid looked at me open-mouthed and said, "Wow! I don't know if I would have done that." I just shook my head. I doubt I would have done that either. I'm afraid my reaction might have been, "Thank You, Lord, for this great blessing. I'll get myself a motorcycle and make good time in serving You."

Ernesto's response was different. He immediately thought of others and how the money could serve as many as possible.

Isn't it a blessing to hear the story of someone with so little, whose first thought—when given something of value—is *How can I use this blessing to bless others*? That's a legacy builder right there! And consider this: Ernesto's sacrifice continues to bless people each time I tell his story!

When we give that which is meaningful and valuable, our sacrifice validates our original intention in trying to leave a lasting legacy: love. Sacrifice is the culmination of our original desire to help others with no thought of reward.

QUESTIONS FOR REFLECTION

1. Do you begin each day with a clear objective? Are you more proactive or reactive?
2. Who do you admire because of his or her ability to stay focused on what matters?
3. Most people have dreams and goals. What makes it hard to put our ideas into action?
4. Are you more of a dreamer or a doer? What are the pros and cons of each personality?
5. Why do you think some people sacrifice so effortlessly for others while others struggle with being generous?
6. Think about the kind of legacy you'd like to leave and rate yourself on a scale from 1–10 (1 = *I'm going nowhere!* and 10 = *I'm making incredible progress!*) in each of these areas:

Being intentional	1	2	3	4	5	6	7	8	9	10
Taking action	1	2	3	4	5	6	7	8	9	10
Being sacrificial	1	2	3	4	5	6	7	8	9	10

8

WHY IT STICKS

> Integrity is not a 90 percent thing, not a 95 percent thing; either you have it or you don't.
>
> Peter Scotese

Although this quality comes last in our list of traits that are vital for building a good and lasting legacy, no one should conclude it is less important than the other five. Many a legacy has collapsed because this one trait was missing. A lasting legacy is . . .

Supported by a Lifestyle of Integrity

What do we mean when we use the word *integrity*? It's the state of being complete, sound, consistent, whole, entire, unimpaired, undivided.

When you ponder all our English words similar to *integrity*, you begin to grasp the beauty and importance of this character quality. An *integer* is a whole number, not a fraction. *Integration* is bringing diverse parts into a unified whole. An *integral* engine part is essential—if it's missing, the engine won't run; it will be impaired. To *disintegrate* is to break apart.

Thus to have integrity is to be wholly—not mostly—moral. People of integrity don't have a "split personality" when it comes to behavior. They don't have a public persona and a private persona. They're consistent. Their beliefs and behaviors are aligned. People of integrity are truthful even when it costs them. They are trustworthy even when no one is watching.

Proverbs 10:9 says, "Whoever walks in integrity walks securely, but whoever takes crooked paths will be found out." This is why we say a good legacy is *supported by a lifestyle of integrity*. The word *support* means to "to uphold or defend as valid or right." That's what integrity does. It supports the legacy we want to leave. Think of how often you hear this tragic story: a trusted leader (perhaps even known for advocating a certain message) gets caught living a contradictory life. In a flash, a reputation built over years comes crashing down, wounding countless others in the process.

Integrity prevents that. Integrity supports and protects. When we are not living a divided, double life, we don't have to fear that at some point we will be revealed.

Before we look at some of the nuances of integrity, let's make sure we say this: *Integrity is not perfection.* We're not perfect people by any means. And we won't be this side of heaven. But God does call us to pursue being wholly holy (not holey). This is something we need to work at every day. The thought of *I'll work on my character and integrity every few months* utterly misses the point.

Let's look more closely at three aspects of integrity.

Honesty. An ancient proverb says, "A liar needs a good memory." Ponder that for a second.

Through the years I've conducted business training for multiple companies. Business leaders get very interested in the subject of integrity when there's a lack of it in their company. In conference rooms all over the country, I have led lengthy discussions of the simple question, "What is a lie?"

Broadly, we can think of a lie as any attempt to deceive. Why is it that when others mislead us, we are quick to label them as liars? But when we are deceptive, we say things like, "Well, I didn't technically say anything that was untrue"? God gave us words to reveal, but we often use them to conceal.

Honesty isn't optional in the Christian life. Larry Burkett put it this way: "A Christian's usefulness to God is directly proportional to his honesty." Why should others believe our message if we're not honest? Only a fool would trust an untrustworthy person . . . which leads us to a second and related component of integrity.

Trustworthiness. How can we know if a person is trustworthy? It's simple: Do they do what they say they will do? It really is that basic.

Do you want to be a person of integrity so that you end up leaving an enduring legacy? Then do this one thing: Do what you say you will do.

But realize that it is possible to be an honest person and not be a trustworthy person. Let me give an example of that. I have a friend who, as far as I know, has never intentionally lied to me. He has never purposely tried to deceive me. And yet he is not trustworthy.

If he called me up and said, "Hey, David, let's grab lunch next Tuesday at noon!" and I agreed, there's a fifty-fifty chance he wouldn't show up. He's absentminded. He simply forgets. He doesn't stand me up with any malice. In fact, he is always sincere (and profuse) in his apologies.

I've gently confronted him several times: "You don't understand how your failure to come through impacts the people around you. People really like you. But when you don't do what you say, they're reluctant to follow you."

Trustworthiness is critical. If you say you're going to do something, do it. Why? Because your personal credibility is at stake and, with that, your ability to influence others. As a business consultant, I often remind leaders that people are watching them and noting what they say, and then what they do (or don't do).

The same goes for you. People—your family members, neighbors, coworkers, students, teammates—are listening to what comes out of your lips and looking at what takes place in your life. They are constantly evaluating whether you are an honest person. A trustworthy person. A "whole" person.

Wholeness. When we talk about wholeness, we are talking about what Proverbs 11:3 teaches: "The integrity of the upright guides them, but the unfaithful are destroyed by their duplicity."

Duplicity is having a public face and a private face; it's when someone demonstrates and promotes a particular set of values at work or school every day, and then lives very differently in other settings. If you live that way, it's likely you will be found out. Here's how author Nathaniel Hawthorne described that dilemma: "No man, for any considerable period, can wear one face to himself, and another to the multitude, without finally getting bewildered as to which may be the true."

Remember my earlier story about my daughter asking why I was always so grumpy when I returned from my speaking engagements? I had a choice in that moment: Am I going to be a man who stands up in front of others and exudes kindness and patience and gentleness . . . but then goes home and barks at his family? Or am I going to live at home in such a way that my wife and children can say, "He practices what he preaches. All that stuff he talks about in public, he lives out in private"? Please don't think I've mastered the art of ungrumpiness (Is that even a word?), but I'm making progress. Asking God for guidance makes a difference. Years ago, God gave me the idea to spend time on my return flight thinking about the encouragement my family needs. That's my habit now, and I thank God for that.

The respect of my wife and children means more to me than anything a stranger could ever say. I'd rather have the confidence and trust of my family than a standing ovation from a packed auditorium. But to cultivate that kind of integrity, I need the help of Christ, the one who was broken so that I could be made whole.

It's encouraging to know that our broken lives can be restored. The Bible provides clear examples of people who once made horrible choices but still managed to leave a great legacy for God's glory. King David, adulterer and murder, is known as "a man after God's own heart" (from Acts 13:22). The apostle Peter publically denied Christ, but Jesus gave him leadership in the early church (from John 21:17). The list could go on and on. Aren't you grateful God gives second (and third) chances? I am. If you lack wholeness, perhaps today is the day you turn to God, repent, and ask Him to guide your steps every day.

Barnabas's lasting legacy as an encourager was supported by his lifestyle of integrity. How do I know he possessed integrity? Because the Bible says this about him: "Barnabas was a good man, full of the Holy Spirit and strong in faith. And many people were brought to the Lord" (Acts 11:24 NLT).

In this context, "good" doesn't mean "above average" or "just short of being great." Goodness is a moral attribute. It's fruit of the Holy Spirit, the character of someone who is indwelt by God himself.

Apart from God, our lives disintegrate. But when we, like Barnabas, are yielded to the Lord, He integrates our lives. He brings our lives into conformity with His. More and more we experience wholeness, and that opens doors for us to tell others about how good the Lord is. And that helps us build a meaningful legacy.

QUESTIONS FOR REFLECTION

1. How would you explain *integrity* to a third grader?
2. The principle in Proverbs 10:9 is that a life of integrity leads to security. What examples of this have you seen?

3. Think about the components of integrity—honesty, trustworthiness, and wholeness—and rate yourself on a scale from 1–10 (1 = *I know that I'm leading a double life* and 10 = *I'm constantly and prayerfully working to be consistently holy*) in each of these areas:

Honesty	1	2	3	4	5	6	7	8	9	10
Trustworthiness	1	2	3	4	5	6	7	8	9	10
Wholeness	1	2	3	4	5	6	7	8	9	10

4. What can a person do, practically and specifically, to cultivate integrity in life?

EXERCISE: The Foundation of a Lasting Legacy

Spend some time reflecting on the six foundational traits for a lasting legacy. In the space provided, you might wish to journal your thoughts. You may want to jot down questions. Whatever God brings to mind, use this time to assess your heart and to ask God to do the transforming work in you that only He can do.

Motivated by LOVE

A deep, tender, indescribable feeling of affection and concern toward a person

____

____

Guided by PASSION

Boundless enthusiasm

Focused by INTENTION

An aim or objective that guides action

Reinforced by ACTION

The good intentions of our heads and hearts carried out by our hands and feet

Confirmed by SACRIFICE

The yielding of something meaningful for the sake of another

____

____

____

____

Supported by a Lifestyle of INTEGRITY

To hold in position so as to keep from falling, sinking, or slipping

____

____

____

____

FURTHER REFLECTION

Of these six traits, which is the strongest in you? Be encouraged by the progress you've made.

____

____

____

Which needs the most improvement? List some practical steps for implementing change:

PART 3

BUILDING A LEGACY

9

LOOKING BACK AND LOOKING FORWARD

> This is the true joy in life, the being used for a purpose recognized by yourself as a mighty one.
>
> George Bernard Shaw

We've seen that a legacy is what we leave behind for others. And we've noted that each of us will move through this life and leave something in our wake: either a memorable history of honoring God and blessing others . . . or a regrettable legacy of damage or lost opportunity.

In part 2 of this book, we explored six traits that provide the foundation for a lasting and positive legacy. One of those is that we must be "focused by intention." That's another way of saying that great legacies don't come about by accident.

This chapter will be highly intentional and practical. In order to identify exactly what you wish to leave behind, you'll need to take a look back . . . and a look forward.

Looking Back

If you've achieved anything good from your life so far (and no doubt you have!), it's because someone took an interest in you and helped you along the way. As I've noted, the most significant people in my life have been my parents and my wife. However, a number of other people—far too many to list—have also played a role in shaping me.

I want to tell you about two individuals who helped me immensely (one personally and the other professionally). You'll notice that neither one was part of my life for a long period of time, yet I can't imagine my life without their investment.

Coach Roberts. In the summer of 1972, my young life was in major upheaval. The previous year, my dad had felt God's call to be a pastor. So he left his job as a chemical engineer and took our family on an "adventure." We relocated from a small town to a big city 250 miles away.

Little did I know at that time the long-term ripple effect that one decision would have on me. (When you're 12, it's not so easy to understand such mysteries.) Even a year after our move, my life and soul were still unsettled. Mostly I missed my friends.

My mom must have sensed my loneliness, so she signed me up for Little League Baseball. Since it was my last year of eligibility, I had grandiose visions of dominating all those younger kids. Because of my age, I was certain I'd be superior to all the others. Was I ever wrong!

First, not having played baseball for a year meant my tryout was a disaster. Second, I got stuck on the worst team in the league. (Due to my abysmal tryout, I was probably the last kid drafted.)

We finished the season with a record of 2 wins and 18 losses. But you know what? It didn't matter. I loved my team, my coach, and the way my game improved every week. In fact, just before our final game, I learned I had actually made the all-star team—something that had never happened to me.

At the end of the regular season, for two full weeks—Monday through Saturday, morning and afternoon—we practiced under the watchful eye of Coach Wiggins. Though he was a stern and humorless man, I got the definite sense he knew what he was doing. After all, it was his team that had won the regular season championship. Coach Wiggins was confident and driven to win.

During my first week of practice, I learned all sorts of new hitting, fielding, and base running techniques. The most interesting tip was how to use my body to stop infield grounders. This was a revelation. Third base had long been my specialty. I had always used my glove when someone hit the ball my way. Now Coach Wiggins wanted me to use my body to stop a screaming ground ball. *Okay,* I thought, *I'll do it for the sake of the team but I don't have to like it.* Sure enough, we did fielding drills without our gloves. Coach made us stop grounders with our sternums, our bellies, our ribs, whatever. He yelled at us repeatedly: "Keep the baseball in front of you!" That's when it hit me (pun intended) that baseball isn't always fun. Still, it seemed like it was worth it, because by the end of the first week I was told that if I continued to perform well, I'd be the starting all-star third baseman.

The second week of practice my dreams of baseball glory began to unravel. On Monday morning I cleanly fielded a grounder near third base (using my glove rather than my chest) and threw to Jack, our first baseman. He would have easily caught it, except that Jack was not eleven feet tall. The ball sailed over his head and crashed loudly into a car parked along the outfield foul line. I quickly learned that this was Coach Wiggins's treasured Ford Woody station wagon. He muttered something under his breath and sent me to the outfield.

I'd never played the outfield. It was halfway to Siberia. From out there, the batter and catcher looked like dots. At the time I didn't know if I was being punished temporarily or banished permanently for hitting my coach's beloved vehicle. Even if my dream of starting at third base was over, that cloud had a silver lining: at least I was far away from Coach Wiggins.

But it was that setback that introduced me to the coach for the outfielders, Coach Roberts. I liked him instantly. Not only did he know my name, he was positive, fun, and quite knowledgeable about the game. Because of him, the rest of that practice week was the most fun I've ever had playing baseball. Whether we were fielding, running the bases, or hitting, he constantly encouraged us.

I remember being in the batting cage one day, trying in vain to hit a curveball. I would have given up, except that Coach Roberts believed in me. "It'll come," he insisted. "Don't give up. You're going to get it!" he urged. Then he stayed after practice to help me get it. He threw curveball after curveball to me. It took over an hour, but I still remember my shock when things began to click. When I began making consistent contact, we celebrated like I'd hit a walk-off home run in game seven of the World Series! After just a few practices with Coach Roberts, my confidence had returned.

At the final practice before our first all-star game, it was announced I would start in right field. I was stunned. I had only been playing the position for a week. I knew I owed all my success to Coach Roberts. Even Coach Wiggins noticed my improvement and complimented me. (Apparently, since I could now hit a curveball, he no longer cared that I had hit his vintage station wagon.)

Our first game was against another Georgia team. It was a classic pitching duel. I came to bat in the second inning and didn't get near the ball. Some pitchers throw curveballs, but this guy threw *curveballs*! I was not alone in my futility. This kid made our whole team look foolish at the plate.

In the final inning, we were down 1–0, and Mr. Curveball had a no-hitter going against us. When I realized I was scheduled to bat third, it occurred to me that I'd likely make the final out of the game. Sure enough, two quick outs and I was headed to the plate. When I was about halfway to the batter's box, Coach Wiggins called me back. He wanted a pinch hitter to replace me, and he yelled for another player to get ready to bat. Secretly I was relieved, thankful I wouldn't be the one to make the last out.

Then, Coach Roberts suddenly emerged and urged Coach Wiggins not to take me out. This was not a welcomed suggestion. Coach Wiggins snapped that his chosen pinch hitter would give us a better shot. And I silently agreed with him.

Coach Roberts, however, was adamant. I think everyone in the ballpark was stunned to see such a passionate plea from an assistant coach. He forcefully told Coach Wiggins he knew I would come through. I remember looking up at my mom in the stands and shrugging. Finally Coach Wiggins relented. He called me over. "Get on base." Then he walked away. In all my years of watching baseball, I've never seen an assistant coach plead like that with the head coach—on the field!—on behalf of a player.

I was flattered that Coach Roberts believed in me, but I felt a lot of pressure. I could hear his encouragement coming from first base. His confidence built my confidence. I was determined to get on base.

The first pitch was just a bit outside, but I hit it hard and foul. My confidence was growing. The next pitch was inside and I fouled it off. Down to my last strike, I was ready when that third pitch came. It was on the outside part of the plate, my favorite location.

I'll never know if I would have hit the ball or not. My bat hit the catcher's mitt. I stood there stunned, not sure what to do. I had no idea what the ruling would be. The umpire called catcher's interference and awarded me first base. Fittingly I stood on first base beside Coach Roberts. The game ended with a strikeout of the next batter. I was the only player on base for our team that day.

We lost the game but I received something far greater. I only later realized all that Coach Roberts did for me that day. It wasn't just that he stood up for me. He believed in me when I didn't believe much in myself. He forced me to face my struggles and do something I didn't want to do. Even if I had struck out, I still would have had that powerful lesson.

Underlying his encouragement was a fact I couldn't deny: he was for me. He wanted me to be successful. He saw potential in me and worked with me to get better. He cared enough to let me face challenges that would make me better. And he would be there for me no matter the result.

Does this sound familiar to you? Have you had someone in your personal life who was for you?

Mallard. My first job lasting more than two weeks was at B. Dalton Bookseller in Greenbrier Mall in Atlanta, Georgia. I was 16 years old and didn't have a clue what I was doing. Sure, I had heard of these rectangular objects called "books." In school, I had even read a handful—the so-called classics, forced upon unsuspecting, uncultured students like myself by teachers trying to exercise their intellectual superiority.

As it turned out, working in a bookstore changed the way I viewed books, and I actually developed a lifelong love of reading. However, while I learned all about books in my first three months, I didn't learn much about customer interaction, and I remained a socially awkward teen. That changed when Mallard became our new store manager. Over the next year my people skills increased dramatically. Why? Because of how I saw Mallard interact with people.

First, he took an interest in his staff and asked specific, genuine questions about each person's life and dreams. He would rotate his schedule so he could spend time with each team member. When he asked you a question, you could tell he was truly listening. This was all he did the first two months or so. Then he started making suggestions for improvement. By this point, I took everything he said to heart. He made recommendations about how to interact with customers. He modeled what he was recommending so I was never lacking in examples. After a year, my customer skills were much improved and my confidence was soaring.

Mallard's management skills impacted me immensely. What he did was so simple, yet it was highly effective:

- He took a genuine interest in each team member.
- He listened.
- He adjusted his schedule to spend time with each team member.
- He knew the business, but he continued to learn more.
- He modeled the right behavior.

And because of all that . . .

- He made suggestions that were readily embraced.

Subconsciously, I began to emulate Mallard's model. It wasn't until years later that I was able to articulate exactly what he did. Now I try to pass on this same model to others. I know I'll never approach Mallard's skill level, but I'm grateful for his legacy and impact.

Those are two of my stories. What are some of yours?

EXERCISE: The Specific Impact of Others on Your Life

Take a few moments to look back over your life. Then, in the space below, name some of the key people who have been role models to you. What examples, traits, life lessons, and so on did they give to you or model for you that you want to pass on to others? List at least one lasting legacy of each person.

PERSONAL Life

Example: My mother—She was never in a hurry. She rarely got impatient or flustered. She lived in the moment—in fact, she enjoyed the moment!

1.

____

____

2.

____

____

3.

PROFESSIONAL Life

Example: I have a long-term associate and friend, Walt, who has helped me in these areas:

- *Excellence*
- *Value of fun and laughter*
- *The joy of giving*
- *A heart to serve others*

He has modeled these traits for me consistently for over 20 years. And these are traits that I value so much that I want to cultivate them and pass them on to others.

1.

2.

3.

Looking Forward

Not only do we have people who have helped us in life but we are surrounded by people who need help. The challenge before us is to realize that these are people *we* can help.

Who are those specific people in your life? It's likely a short list. Jesus mostly focused on impacting twelve students (so that they could and would turn around and do the same for others).

I've discovered that the best way to know the identity of the people God wants me to serve is to ask Him. He might direct your attention to a family member or a neighbor. Maybe a kid you are teaching or coaching. Maybe a single mom who needs a helping hand. Maybe that person no one else notices. Maybe someone at work. Spend time in prayer asking God to show you whom He wants you to come alongside and encourage.

EXERCISE: The Specific Impact of My Life on Others

In the space below, take a few moments to name some of the people God has already put in your life or path (and on your heart). Keep in mind that you may want to add to this list later. You may even decide to prioritize your list. But for now, start with those to whom you are the closest (family, friends), then move outward to consider others in your sphere of influence.

PERSONAL Life

Example: My son—he's 10 and in the fourth grade. I have about eight more years with him before he leaves the nest.

1.

____

____

____

2.

____

____

____

3.

____

____

____

PROFESSIONAL Life

Example: My intern—she's a college student working in our office for the next three months, and this is a great opportunity to model a strong work ethic for her.

1.

____

____

____

2.

____

____

____

3.

____

____

____

QUESTIONS FOR REFLECTION

1. What names and faces pop into your mind and make you smile when you think back over your life?

2. If it's true that God is sovereign—that is, that nothing in life is accidental or beyond His plans and purposes—what do your current relationships and social networks tell you about the people He would have you influence?

10

YOUR INTERESTS AND VALUES

> Ask yourself what makes you come alive and then go do that. Because what the world needs is people who have come alive.
>
> Howard Thurman

The legacies we leave always revolve around our interests and values.

The man or woman who is obsessed with stockpiling wealth will be remembered as a money-grubber. The person who lavishes his or her energy, abilities, and resources on loving and serving others will be remembered as a treasured friend.

We will consider interests and values separately. However, as we begin, tuck this truth away: When noble interests and God-honoring values align with deliberate actions, the result is the kind of legacy that is both breathtaking and lasting.

Interests

Your interests are your passions—the people, activities, and things that make you come alive. Often, these interests are reflected in our hobbies and in how we spend our free time. Where does your mind tend to drift when it's not occupied with urgent have-tos? What are your get-tos? That's a good indicator of your interests and passions.

I have twin nephews, Rob and Jimmy. I was at the hospital the day they were born. Truth be told, they were red and scrawny (and frankly looked like little aliens). Later, when they were young, they tended to be a bit on the wild side ("wild" is probably too mild a term). Anyway, they grew out of their alien looks and hooligan actions and matured into fine young men. They hold a very special place in my heart.

One of them, Rob, was working for the Secret Service at one of the World Trade Center buildings on September 11, 2001. There was a period of time when we didn't know if he was okay. Thankfully, he not only survived the 9/11 attacks, he helped a number of others escape from the Twin Towers (though he inhaled a lot of smoke in the process).

His brother, Jimmy, decided he wanted to do something to serve his country, so he joined the Marines. While he was in officer's training school, he wrote my father—his grandfather—this letter:

Dear Grandpa,

A funny thing happened last week when my unit was qualifying with an M16A2 rifle on the rifle range.

I had been shooting well all week, and at the 200-yard line on qualification day I shot reasonably well. However, at the 300-yard line I shot far below par—meaning I found myself at the 500-yard line, needing eight of ten shots in the black.

Just then the wind picked up. I made a wind call to compensate, but the wind was probably 5 mph greater than I judged. I missed my first shot by about 4–5 inches. I was discouraged—I would have to put nine of the next ten shots in the black from 500 yards away! I adjusted accordingly, but at 500 yards with an open sight, the head and torso of a man is rather small. Then, just before I took my next shot, something occurred to me—that dime that you, Rob, and I used to shoot at with our .22 caliber Marlin is even smaller than a man's silhouette at 500 yards! Encouraged by that memory, I hit nine of my next ten shots and qualified as a rifle expert!

I wanted to take this opportunity to thank the man who taught me how to shoot a rifle as a boy. Please accept this US Marine Corps shooting badge as a token of my appreciation for the first rifle expert I ever knew—my grandpa. If memory serves me correctly, you are still the title holder for our dime-shooting competition.

I'm so thankful for the time you invested in me when I was young, and I know my brother feels the same way.

Your grandson,
Jimmy, second lieutenant, United States Marine Corps

My dad had that letter and the shooting badge framed and put on his wall. It is a sweet reminder of all the times he spent with his young grandsons. My dad loved shooting guns, fishing, camping, and watching Clint Eastwood movies, among other things. My point is this: He used his interests to spend time with others.

Our interests are an easy and natural way to connect with the people we love and want to influence. I believe God gives us interests and hobbies not only to encourage and refresh us but also to be a platform from which we can connect with others. For example, a love for baseball allowed me to reconnect with my brother Kevin as an adult. That trip to Cooperstown spurred a deep friendship that we missed as children, and he became one of my closest friends.

EXERCISE: My Unique Hobbies and Interests

Take a few moments for personal reflection. Then, in the space below, list the things you like to do. Include all your favorite hobbies and special interests.

Examples: Gardening, travel, going to the movies, fishing, playing sports, sewing, bird-watching, watching movies, working on cars, going to plays or museums.

____

____

____

Now list the people groups you are drawn to help. Include individuals or groups that have a special place in your heart

Examples: Children or children in my Sunday school class, teens or my teenagers and their friends, elderly, people with physical or emotional needs, young professionals, single dads

____

____

____

Values

At the risk of stating the obvious, our values are the principles or standards that we consider valuable—whatever we deem worthwhile or desirable. Milton Rokeach said that a value is an "enduring belief about the way things should be done, or about the ends we desire."

Since our values always drive our behavior, other people end up being impacted by our personal values. Jesus put it this way: "For where your treasure is, there your heart will be also" (Matthew 6:21). In other words, our hearts naturally attach to whatever we consider most important. Take a few minutes to wrestle with the question, *What are my true values?*

The following exercise can help clarify your values and narrow your legacy.

EXERCISE: The Deep Values and Burdens of My Heart

In the Bible, we read the remarkable story of a civil servant named Nehemiah who left his home in Shushan, Persia, and traveled 750 miles to the city he had never seen before but that meant so much to him and his Jewish compatriots. The city of Jerusalem was in ruins, and Nehemiah went there to rebuild its ancient walls. After a long journey, Nehemiah said, "I had not told anyone what my God had put in my heart to do for Jerusalem" (Nehemiah 2:12).

Why did Nehemiah leave his comfort zone of Shushan? Because of what God put on his heart to do for others.

Take some time to think over the following questions:

- What do I believe in?
- What am I passionate about?
- What do I stand for?
- What do I really care about?
- What burden has God placed on my heart?

These are not easy questions. They will require time in soul-searching thought and prayer. These questions can be convicting when they reveal that we have become enamored with trivial things. Answering these questions gives us a clearer picture of what truly matters to us.

Let me encourage you to get alone and ask God to answer these questions with and for you. Ultimately, the legacies with the most enduring impact are the ones that have been directed by God.

____

____

____

____

____

Follow-up suggestion: If you are brave enough, you can get an even clearer perspective into what values motivate you by asking close friends and trusted loved ones to answer those same questions based on what they know of your character and actions.

QUESTIONS FOR REFLECTION

1. Does it seem strange to you (or somehow like "cheating") that God would want to use your interests, fun

hobbies, and enjoyable activities to help you leave a positive legacy?
2. What should we do about our values that are not exactly noble?
3. Can you think of specific ways some of your values have changed over time for the better?

11

NARROWING YOUR LEGACY

> Remember, O my God, all that I have done for these people, and bless me for it.
>
> Nehemiah

A legacy is whatever we leave behind for others. That legacy can be remarkable or regrettable. It can be lasting or quickly forgotten. In this short book, we're looking at how to leave a worthy, enduring legacy—a legacy that both honors God and blesses others.

In the last couple of chapters, we've begun the process of zeroing in on the unique impact God would have *you* make on this world. In the next few pages, you will attempt to spell that out.

EXERCISE: Narrowing Your Legacy

Based on the unique interests and values you identified in the last chapter, what do you want to leave behind for others? Your big, overall legacy will be comprised of smaller elements, and those can be anything that glorifies God and brings good to others.

As you consider the people on whom you want to make a positive and lasting impact, list five specific legacies you'd like to leave.

Example: I want to be known as a person of ________ [faith, honesty, courage, humility, integrity, encouragement, compassion, love, humor, justice, persistence, etc.]

I want to be known as a person who ________ [solved problems, was a loving parent/spouse/friend, was a peacemaker, was adaptable, etc.]

1.

____

____

____

2.

____

____

3.

____

____

4.

____

____

5.

____

____

Of your five responses, what is the one trait or quality for which you *most* want to be remembered? Why?

Answering this "Why?" question reveals our true motivation for wanting to leave a legacy. I love what Nehemiah said after Jerusalem's walls were rebuilt: "Remember, O my God, all that I have done for these people, and bless me for it" (Nehemiah 5:19 NLT). Notice he didn't say, "Remember me as a gifted leader who helped my people rebuild walls that had been down for decades." He didn't say, "Remember my meteoric rise from humble civil servant to governor of the land." He humbly said, "Lord, remember me for all I have done for your people." This statement reveals why he was willing to travel so far to rebuild a devastated city: *he did it for others.*

EXERCISE: Making It Happen

You obviously want to forge a life of impact—otherwise you would have closed this book by now.

You have identified the one legacy piece that you feel the greatest nudge of God to begin cultivating.

Now brainstorm how you can begin to see that realized in your life. Engage in a little "sanctified daydreaming." Come up with five specific actions that could get you rolling:

Example: I could form a book club or small group and work through this book with several friends.

1.

____

____

____

2.

____

____

____

3.

____

____

____

4.

____

____

____

5.

____

____

____

If you're having a hard time thinking of anything specific, let me share some of my secrets. These are tools I use to help me be intentional in building a lasting legacy.

1. Prayer

We know that prayer is vital to our walk with Jesus. Oswald Chambers said, "Prayer does not equip us for greater works—prayer *is* the greater work." Prayer is the single most important thing we can do in this whole process of seeking to leave a lasting legacy. Nothing is more important. The more we commune with Christ, the more we hear what He has to say. That's how we know what He wants us to leave for the sake of others.

2. Creative Visual Reminders

Without a doubt, God has called me to be an encourager of people. Several years ago, I typed the word ENCOURAGE on a card, laminated it, and stuck it in my computer bag where I'd see it often. I also attached an identical card to my computer screen at work and left it there for about six months. Since I am a visual person, every time I saw those cards, I was reminded of my life mission.

In part 1 of *Your Legacy*, I shared my story about the baseball bat that people sign for me. That exercise is always a wonderful opportunity to sit down with people who have impacted my life, share what they mean to me, and have them autograph my bat. This bat hangs in my office, and I'll treasure it for the rest of my days. My dad and mom are no longer with me, but seeing their signatures is a beautiful reminder that all I've been given needs to be passed on to the next generation.

There is tremendous motivation in having visual reminders of the impact that others have had on you—or the impact that you want to have on others.

3. The Involvement of Others

Find a trusted confidant or two—perhaps your spouse or a close, trusted friend—who can hear you out and give you feedback. This is important because others can often see the hand of God in your life in ways that you can't. My wife, Pam, is that person for me, and I'm that person for her. Find someone you can engage with in that way. Show or tell them about the things you are working on: "These are some of the ways I think God wants me to have a lasting impact on others. What do you think about this?"

4. Accountability

Do you remember the story about my daughter calling me "grumpy"? That incident shook me in deep ways. But a lot of good resulted from it. One benefit was increased accountability.

Pam had been warning me about overcommitting and traveling too much. It was that experience that made me really see this blind spot in my life. Upon reflection, I realized I had a problem turning down ministry or consulting opportunities. I couldn't say no to people who wanted me to speak or consult. Part of this was driven by the fear I wouldn't be asked again. Part of it was my own ego.

Out of this experience with my daughter, Pam and I set up an arrangement in which she has complete veto power over any invitation I receive to speak. I tell groups now that if they've enjoyed (or despised!) my teaching—it's all because of Pam Hodge. She tells me where, when, and to whom I can speak.

Pam guards me from trying to do too much. She can see the big picture, especially concerning my energy levels. And if I start getting grumpy, I have authorized her to tell me about it. Believe me, she does! This accountability has been very helpful.

If you're serious about what you want to leave behind, get a "checker." Everyone needs a checker of some type, a trusted ally who can speak the truth in love to you. Accountability will help you grow. It will broaden and deepen the legacy you want to leave.

Let's conclude this chapter with another practical exercise.

EXERCISE: Getting Specific

Begin listing very detailed ways your primary legacy goal can become more of a reality, including improving on what you are already doing. Remember, there are no wrong answers. Simply brainstorm some concrete ways to fulfill your legacy goals.

Where possible, write out more detailed plans or outline specific steps that you can take to begin implementing these ideas immediately.

Example: Since I want to be an intentional parent, I will:

1. *Plan a weekly "date" with each of my two children.*
2. *Pray with both of my kids every single night at bedtime.*
3. *Begin saving for a special trip with each of my kids when they turn 13.*

1.

____

____

2.

____

____

3.

____

____

4.

____

____

5.

____

____

QUESTIONS FOR REFLECTION

1. What have you found most difficult in this process of attempting to be more intentional about leaving a certain legacy?
2. In general, what's more difficult for you—coming up with a realistic plan or carrying out a plan? Why do you think that is?
3. So far, what has surprised you most as you have worked through the material and exercises in this book?

12

STAYING ON THE PATH

> When a man does not know what harbor he is making for, no wind is the right wind.
>
> Seneca

In chapter 4, we discussed the ways a legacy is like the baton in a relay race. Passing that baton takes focus and skill.

We've seen the importance of forgiveness and gratitude in receiving whatever legacy the previous generation has given to us. We looked at the importance of sure footing as we run the race of life, and we covered the six traits that will provide that.

Now it's time to begin the process of passing the baton to those who will follow after us. This hand-off calls for planning. We have to be extremely intentional. Why is it necessary to think about such things *today*? Because none of us knows how much longer we'll be around. That's not meant to scare you; it's merely a reminder of biblical truth (see Psalm 139:16). God has ordained for each of us a finite number of days. You won't get any less than God has ordained; you won't get any more.

As we wrestle with such matters, it's helpful to again focus on Jesus (like we did back in chapter 3). The Son of God left the greatest legacy ever. He clearly understood why He came to earth, and He was able to articulate what He hoped to leave behind: "I came not to be served but to serve and to give my life as a ransom for many." The ultimate Servant, Jesus wanted to pass on this trait to His followers.

The Gospels and the book of Acts show us that this is exactly what happened. In the New Testament, we see three discernable actions that Jesus took that ensured His disciples would receive His legacy of servanthood with all of their hearts.

In his earthly ministry, Jesus made lots of astounding statements. Puzzling statements, like "the last will be first, and the first will be last" (Matthew 20:16). His teaching is even more stunning when you expect Him to say certain things . . . and He doesn't. When His disciples argued among themselves over which one was the greatest, for instance. My expectation of Jesus is that He would have responded, "You shouldn't want that—that's arrogant!" But Jesus never said that. In essence He told His followers, "If you want to be great, fine. But understand the path to true greatness" (see Matthew 18:1–4; 20:20–24; Luke 22:24–30).

It's incredible to me that one of these arguments among the disciples took place during the Last Supper! This was an emotional, highly charged few hours. He had been with them constantly for three years, pouring His life into their lives, but now He was talking about leaving them. He took the bread that was in front of Him and said, "This bread represents my body, which will be broken for you." Next He took the cup of wine and said, "You see this fruit of the vine? This represents the blood that I'm about to shed for you." What a powerful, unforgettable moment! The Son of God is telling His most intimate associates, "I'm going to die . . . for you."

Immediately after this stirring, emotional revelation, the Bible says, "A dispute also arose among them as to which of them was considered to be greatest" (Luke 22:24). Talk about a group of oblivious people! Again I'm intrigued by the fact that Jesus does not rebuke them.

Instead of exhibiting anger or frustration, telling His disciples their dispute was ill-timed or inappropriate, Jesus shows great restraint. He gently instructs them about servant leadership. He notes how "the kings of the Gentiles lord it over" their subjects. This is a very powerful response. He's basically saying that most worldly leaders overwhelm others by their power. "But you are not to be like that," Jesus declared. "Instead, the greatest among you should be like the youngest, and the one who rules like the one who serves. For who is greater, the one who is at the table or the one who serves? Is it not the one who is at the table? But I am among you as one who serves" (Luke 22:25–27).

Things really haven't changed since Jesus's time. Most people view the "greater" as the person who can bark an order and have "lesser" underlings run to and fro to satisfy his or her every whim.

But did you catch what Jesus said? "I am among you as one who serves." True greatness, lasting greatness, is found when we sign up to serve, not scramble to serve.

I travel a lot in my job. So I spend a lot of time at Hartsfield-Jackson Atlanta International, the world's busiest airport. Every time I'm there I see dazed and confused people who clearly need help finding their way.

Recently I saw a woman who looked overwhelmed. "Can I help you?" I asked. The relief on her face was instantaneous.

"Yes!" she said. "I need to find the MARTA train. Can you point it out to me?"

"I'll do better than that. I'll take you there."

She and I had a nice conversation, and I got her headed to her destination. Afterwards I was reminded that it's the simple, little things that really represent Jesus to others. And I need to be far more intentional about that. In this one powerful moment, when Jesus had His disciples' attention, He says in effect, "The great people on this earth lord it over you, but I am among you as one who serves. And I want you to be people who serve others. Be people who ask, 'How can I help you?'"

STEP 1: Prioritize It.

How did Jesus pass on this legacy of servanthood? First, He prioritized it. That is to say, because it was important to Him, it was kept on the front burner throughout His ministry. This is seen in how often He talked about serving others and how often he modeled it.

If we don't prioritize what matters most to us, we'll have a tendency to delay it or even forget it. The Bible uses the word "remember" over two hundred times (often in reference to what God has done for us). Why? Because our tendency is to forget. We need to be intentional about keeping it a priority.

Years ago, my dad helped me understand the power of prioritizing the most important matters in life. A little backstory is necessary. My dad became a follower of Christ when he was 30 years old and I was just a little kid. His was a dramatic conversion, and his life changed quickly and profoundly. My mom told me that every Sunday for over a decade as she loaded my older siblings and me in the family station wagon, she would ask my dad to attend church with her. And every Sunday for over a decade, my dad refused. Then, suddenly, one Sunday he said yes. After years of asking, my mom's prayers were realized. Not only did my dad attend, he surrendered his life to Christ that day.

To say my dad was enthusiastic about his faith in Christ would be a gross understatement. He loved Jesus, and everyone he encountered experienced that love through his words, actions, and clothing choices. (He was fond of Jesus-slogan ties and T-shirts.) Remarkably, he was the least offensive person I've ever known.

About 25 years after my dad's conversion, I was hired to teach Greek and New Testament at a Christian college. I called my dad to tell him about it, and he was so very pleased. He kept telling me how proud he was of me, that in his wildest dreams he never imagined he would have a son who would do that.

So I began teaching Greek. But after three years, I was absolutely sick of it! Frankly, it bored me, but I had to study it daily in order to teach with excellence. I wanted desperately to quit, but I hesitated. Inwardly, the job was crushing my spirit and I never wanted to see another Greek word, but I couldn't bear the thought of calling my dad to tell him I didn't want to teach at a college anymore.

When it became unbearable, I resigned and I called my dad with the news.

"Dad, I know this disappoints you," I began to explain, but he cut me off. He apologized to me immediately, saying,

"Son, I raised you for one reason and one reason only, and that is to serve God. I'm sorry if I gave you any other impression. I'm proud of you no matter what you do." As soon as he said it, I knew exactly what his and mom's ultimate goal was in raising their four children. My mom and dad simply wanted us to love and serve God. Ultimately, I figured out a way of serving God that is more suited to my God-given abilities and passions. But it took my father's patient support and wise counsel to help me figure that out. That's part of his tremendous legacy, and I do what I do today because of that.

One of the legacies I believe God wants me to leave behind is encouragement. Over the years I realized that I need to be intentional about keeping it a priority. It's possible to have a gift and a calling and then simply forget to utilize it. The next two steps will help keep it a priority.

STEP 2: Mention It.

It would be a shame to have strong beliefs and clear values, but then never mention them to others. How can we pass on a legacy of purity or integrity, for example, if we rarely talk about the importance of those virtues? Jesus talked about His legacy again and again: "The greatest among you will be your servant" (Matthew 23:11). "Whoever wants to be first must be slave of all" (Mark 10:44).

I've been actively speaking and training in companies, conferences, and churches for over 25 years. God has richly blessed me with these opportunities. I've developed a habit with every new group to share that my personal goal is to encourage them. It helps them to understand where I'm coming from and where I'm going—no matter what the topic. And it also holds me accountable to what I'm called to do.

We can't fully know what a person believes until (and unless) he or she openly shares those beliefs. Words clarify. They explain and shed light. We should never assume people intuitively know what is important to us. Our noble actions may intrigue them, but we must *talk* about what we believe if we want to be sure people understand.

One of the hardest moments of my life was taking my daughter to college for the first time. The day before we left, I was thinking, *Man, I don't know if I've told her everything I need to tell her*. So that night I got on my computer and typed out a two-page list of fatherly thoughts.

The next day, when we got in the car, I said, "Honey, I have a few things I want to communicate to you and I've typed them up here. Since I'm going to be driving, how about if you read them one at a time and we discuss them?"

She was probably rolling her eyes (at least internally), but outwardly she didn't balk. She would read an item from my list and I would make additional comments. Every now and then, she'd ask a question.

We stopped around Macon, Georgia, to have lunch. The whole time we were eating, I wondered *What is she thinking? Is she enjoying this . . . or enduring it?* Imagine my surprise when we got back in the car and the first thing she said was, "Hey, Dad, can we finish the list?"

That was pretty cool. I was reminded through this experience to be more proactive with my other kids. A parent's words are of infinite importance.

Of course, merely sharing with others what we believe does not ensure our values will be passed on. In addition to prioritizing our desired legacy and then talking about it explicitly, there must also be alignment between our words and our behavior. We must . . .

STEP 3: Model It.

As the saying goes, talk is cheap. Anyone can say anything. In the end it is personal behavior that confirms what we *truly* believe. Remember the proverbial teenager who said to her parents, "What you *are* screams so loudly, I cannot hear all the empty words you *say*"?

Or think of the person who constantly claims, "I want to leave a legacy of doing excellent work"—but then, day after day, models a slipshod, careless attitude on the job. He or she is unlikely to be praised, emulated, or remembered fondly by others. If anything, the legacy such a person leaves behind is one of "deadbeat" or "hypocrite."

Jesus clearly modeled this trait himself in His legacy of servanthood. In the Upper Room, after He washed the feet of His followers, He returned to His place at the table and said, "Do you understand what I have done for you?" (John 13:12).

Scripture doesn't tell us how the disciples responded, but I'm sure the answer was, "Not really." At the time, I don't think they had a clue about what was going on. Their minds were reeling, straining to grasp Jesus's topsy-turvy, other-worldly views of leadership. All the disciples knew for sure was that no respectable leader in their culture served His followers the way Jesus had just served them. No wonder this vivid model (and these memories) stayed with them always!

"Example is not the main thing in influencing others," Albert Schweitzer once said. "It is the only thing." You know this is true. The people in closest proximity to you keep their eyes on you whether you want them to or not. They notice your behavior. They notice if it matches what you say. The effectiveness of your intended legacy with others is often attached to how consistently your behavior matches your words.

How did Jesus stay on the path for His stated goal to serve others? First, He prioritized it as something God wanted him to be and to do every day. Then he proceeded to teach it and model it for His disciples over a three-year period. It stuck with them, as the New Testament attests, and they became what Jesus intended: individuals who served others in His name and changed the world. I believe the same process will help keep us on the path of leaving a good and lasting legacy.

EXERCISE: Preparing to Pass the Baton

Identify a person you'd like to impact. It could be a son or daughter, a grandchild, a junior associate at work, a kid you're coaching or teaching, or someone from church who's in a younger stage of life. This individual needs to be someone you have regular contact with and who would be favorable to your input into his or her life.

Write the individual's name here:

____

Write the legacy you wish to leave (see chapter 11):

____

____

PRIORITIZE It: Remind yourself how important the legacy process is. Pray, "Lord, not my will, but your will be done." Consider the reasons why leaving a legacy for this person is important to you.

____

____

MENTION It: Write down specific ways you can express it to this person.

____

____

____

MODEL It: Think of concrete ways you can show this person your legacy by your behavior.

____

____

____

QUESTIONS FOR REFLECTION

1. Who have been the primary positive influencers in your life?
2. What are some of the specific ways they influenced you?
3. What lessons, values, or skills did they pass on to you?

13

TIME TO PASS IT ON

> This is our work in creation: to decide. And what we decide is woven into the thread of time and being forever.
>
> Dafyd in *Merlin*

People give many excuses for why they don't seem to be leaving the legacy they want to leave—lack of time, pressures at work, the distractions and struggles of life.

Ultimately, however, there is only one thing that will keep you from having the impact you want to have: *you!* There is no sense in blaming anyone or anything else. Your legacy is in your hands.

It comes down to a decision: Will you choose to implement the legacy plan you've crafted?

In a moment, I'll invite you to actually make a commitment to God to begin, but before we do that, let's focus on the reward of a worthy legacy.

The Reward

I have taken thousands of school teachers through this legacy process, and I've decided there's no group of people on earth that needs encouragement more than teachers. They are a creative bunch—but chronically overworked and underpaid.

Often, I end the seminar by showing the closing scene from the popular 1995 film *Mr. Holland's Opus.* (If you never saw the movie, let me spoil it for you by describing what unfolds.)

Glenn Holland (played wonderfully by Richard Dreyfuss) has always dreamed of composing great orchestral music . . . yet he finds himself working not in the world's great concert halls, but in a shabby high school band room. (Holland stumbled into this career some 25 years before when his artistic pursuits failed to generate an income.)

Holland has never been able to write and publish the music he'd hoped to create for the world. And now it's his last day on the job. School officials are eliminating his department and forcing him to retire.

What Holland doesn't know is that hundreds of his former students have come back to the school to honor him in a surprise appreciation ceremony. When his wife and son lead him into the school auditorium, the packed crowd erupts with cheering and applause. The governor (also a former student) is on hand. She serves as master of ceremonies and tells the stunned Mr. Holland that he might *think* his life was a failure because he never got to do what he really wanted—publish and perform the one great work he did manage to compose—but then she tells him to scan the crowd. Everyone present has been impacted by his life.

As the governor informs Mr. Holland that an orchestra (comprised of his former students) will now play his music publicly for the first time, the curtain opens to reveal a stage full of smiling musicians. Mr. Holland is overwhelmed as he takes the director's baton from the governor. The audience then watches and listens as his former students play the opus beautifully. Mr. Holland beams as tears stream down his face.

As the orchestra plays Mr. Holland's opus, the closing credits appear. That's my cue in seminars to turn off the movie (which always elicits boos from a few in the crowd). But the response is always the same: almost every teacher at the seminar is visibly moved—some weeping even harder than Mr. Holland himself.

I know why. These teachers are witnessing the thing they—and we—desire most . . . confirmation that our lives have made a difference.

I tell my audiences the unpleasant truth that in all likelihood, they will never, this side of heaven, get to experience a scene quite this dramatic. However, for followers of Jesus, there's an experience that's a billion times better than the closing scene of *Mr. Holland's Opus*.

One day Christians will stand before the Lord. Can you imagine that moment? Angels ceaselessly calling to one another, proclaiming that God Almighty is holy, holy, holy!

The promise of Jesus is that if we have been His faithful followers on earth, we will hear the words we most long to hear: "Well done, good and faithful servant!" The speaker will be the One who has loved us from before time began. *That* is our great reward for living an intentional life of faithfulness to God and service to others. And that is more than enough.

So let's get moving. Start building a good and lasting legacy while you still have the opportunity.

EXERCISE: Making a Commitment

One of the sad realities of life is that though we usually have every good intention to do significant and worthwhile things, we often end up doing nothing.

For many people, the problem is feeling overwhelmed. Perhaps you look at all you'd like to leave behind and find yourself paralyzed. You can't get started. All you can think is, *How do I do this? Leaving a legacy is such a gigantic undertaking!*

It's an epic challenge, all right. Perhaps you've heard the enduring question—"How do you eat an elephant?"—and the famous answer—"One bite at a time, of course." So you tackle the legacy challenge the same way you tackle any other big project in life: bit by bit. As an old Chinese proverb states, "The journey of a thousand miles begins with a single step."

Here, the challenge is to make a commitment to God to do the "one thing" that will get you going. If you haven't already done something similar in earlier chapters, I encourage you to:

1. Specify that one thing. Doing "one thing" will give you encouragement and confidence to do more.

Examples:

Write a thank-you note to _______.

Spend time with _______ *and share my values.*

Ask _______ *about a mentoring relationship.*

Create a fund from which I can contribute regularly to _______.

____

____

2. Set a time limit. Specify a date by which you will complete your "one thing."

____

3. Sign your commitment. Remember, this is a commitment between you and God. Since we have already discussed the value of integrity, I'm sure you would never think of not completing your assignment.

___

4. Share your plan with someone else.

The beauty of the simple approach of starting with just one thing is that when you complete that first step, you'll be motivated to continue on to the next thing. Soon you'll sense a kind of internal momentum. Before long, you'll be on your way—cultivating an intentional legacy that will bring honor to God, blessing to others, and joy to your own heart.

Here's one last thing—and this exercise can serve as an incredible motivation. Take a few minutes to ponder and jot down a response to this question: What if you were able to successfully leave the five legacies you indicated that you desire to leave (pages 124–125)? What would be the impact for the kingdom of God, on others, and on your own soul?

___

___

___

____

____

____

QUESTIONS FOR REFLECTION

1. How are you when it comes to making and keeping commitments?
2. What's harder for you—making a decision or living out a decision? Why?
3. What are you feeling as you come to the end of this study? Excitement? Confusion? Something else? (Note: If you're feeling afraid, remember what author Steven Pressfield says in his book *The War of Art*: "Are you paralyzed with fear? That's a good sign. Fear is good. Like self-doubt, fear is an indicator. Fear tells us what we have to do. Remember our rule of thumb: The more scared we are of a work or calling, the more sure we can be that we have to do it.")

A FINAL WORD

We end where we started—with my twofold hope and prayer:

1. That the truths you've gleaned from God's Word in this study of *Your Legacy* have proven to be a tremendous encouragement to you; and
2. That you would turn around and encourage others by putting into practice all you've learned. The goal of information is always transformation. Resist the temptation to keep these biblical principles to yourself. Share them freely—as God directs—by both your words and your actions.

NOTES

The number preceding each citation is the page number where the corresponding quotation can be found.

Chapter 1

15 ***Epigraph:*** Steve Saint and Genny Saint, *Walking His Trail: Signs of God Along the Way* (Carol Stream, IL: Tyndale), xiv.

Chapter 2

21 ***Epigraph:*** Quoted in John R. W. Stott, *Christ and the Media* (Vancouver, BC: Regent College Publishing, 1977), 25

22 ***Meyer:*** Paul J. Meyer, *Unlocking Your legacy: 25 Keys for Success* (Chicago: Moody, 2002), 17.

24 ***Muggeridge:*** Quoted in John R. W. Stott, *Christ and the Media* (Vancouver, BC: Regent College Publishing, 1977), 25.

25 ***Moore:*** Quoted in Dennis Rainey and Barbara Rainey, *The Art of Parenting* (Grand Rapids, MI: Bethany House, 2018), loc. 3890, Kindle.

26 ***Dobson:*** You'll easily find this story online. I originally found it here: Valerie Wells, "Dobson Urged 'End of Life' Test," *Herald & Review*, Decatur, IL, October 5, 1997, B5.

26 ***Wood:*** Paul J. Meyer, *Unlocking Your Legacy: 25 Keys for Success* (Chicago: Moody, 2002), 151.

27 ***Maxwell:*** John C. Maxwell, "Work to Live Your Life Usefully and Success Will Follow," Louisville Business First, January 3, 2005, https://www.bizjournals.com/louisville/stories/2005/01/03/smallb3.html.

27 *"Nobody on his deathbed":* Paul Tsongas, *Heading Home* (New York: Vintage Books, 1992), 160.

Chapter 3

29 *Epigraph:* John W. Gardner, *The Recovery of Confidence* (New York: W. W. Norton, 1971), 52.

30 *Ledbetter:* J. Otis Ledbetter and Kurt Bruner, *Your Heritage: How to Be Intentional about the Legacy You Leave* (1996, Moody Press; 1999, Heritage Builder Books), 230.

31 *Blanchard:* Ken Blanchard and Colleen Barrett, *Lead with LUV: A Different Way to Create Real Success* (Upper Saddle River, NJ: Pearson Education, 2011), 120.

34 *Booth:* Shaw Clifton, "Others," from Letters to the Army, pastoral letter four, October 2007, http://web.salvationarmy.org/ihq/www_ihq_general.nsf/vw-print/423bad8664f55a89802573830082948e!OpenDocument&Click=.

38 *Swindoll:* Charles Swindoll, *Strengthening Your Grip: How to Be Grounded in a Chaotic World*, rev. ed. (Franklin, TN: Worthy, 2015), 227.

38 *Ten Boom:* Corrie ten Boom with Jamie Buckingham, *Tramp for the Lord: The Story That Begins Where the Hiding Place Ends* (Fort Washington, PA: CLC Publications, 1974), 195.

Chapter 4

41 *Epigraph:* Quoted in Paul Fein, *Tennis Confidential II* (Lincoln, NE: Potomac Books, 2009), ix.

44 *Meyer:* Paul J. Meyer, *24 Keys That Bring Complete Success* (Gainesville, FL: Bridge-Logos, 2006), 56.

44 *Smedes:* Lewis B. Smedes, *Forgive and Forget: Healing the Hurts We Don't Deserve* (New York: HarperCollins, 1984, 1996), x.

47 *McCullough:* Jeff Diamant, "Grateful People Are Healthier, Happier, Researchers Say," *Atlanta Constitution*, November 28, 2003, F2.

47 *McAdams:* Jeff Diamant, "Grateful People Are Healthier, Happier, Researchers Say," *Atlanta Constitution*, November 28, 2003, F2.

50 *Gibson:* Quoted in Paul Fein, *Tennis Confidential II* (Lincoln, NE: Potomac Books, 2009), ix.

Chapter 5

57 ***Epigraph:*** Kenneth Boa, *Conformed to His Image: Biblical and Practical Approaches to Spiritual Formation* (Grand Rapids: Zondervan, 2001), 48.

59 ***Teammates:*** David Halberstam (New York, NY: Hachette, 2003), 51–52.

Chapter 6

63 ***Epigraph:*** Rick Warren, *The Purpose Driven Life: What on Earth Am I Here For?* expanded ed. (Grand Rapids, MI: Zondervan, 2002, 2012), 127.

64 ***Haggai:*** John Haggai, *Lead On!* (Waco TX: Word Books, 1986), 46.

66 ***Barkley:*** You can find the 1993 "I Am Not a Role Model" Nike commercial on YouTube.

66 ***Malone:*** Karl Malone, *Sports Illustrated*, "One Role Model to Another," June 14, 1993, https://www.si.com/vault/1993/06/14/128740/one-role-model-to-another-whether-he-likes-it-or-not-charles-barkley-sets-an-example-that-many-will-follow.

67 ***Mother Teresa . . . no better quote:*** Mother Teresa, *Where There Is Love, There Is God: Mother Teresa—Her Path to Closer Union with God and Greater Love for Others*, ed. Brian Kolodiejchuk (New York: Doubleday Religion: 2010), 156.

67 ***Mother Teresa . . . once said:*** Donna-Marie Cooper O'Boyle, *Mother Teresa and Me: Ten Years of Friendship* (Vancouver WA: Circle Press, 2010), 188.

68 ***Martin Luther King Jr.:*** David L. Lewis, *King: A Biography* (Champaign IL: University of Illinois Press, 1978), 390.

68 ***Emerson:*** Ralph Waldo Emerson, "Circles" in *Essays by R. W. Emerson*, First Series, new ed. (Boston: James Munroe and Company, 1850), 292.

69 ***Chariots of Fire:*** Colin Welland (writer) and Hugh Hudson (director), *Chariots of Fire*, motion picture (Burbank, CA: Warner Bros, 1981).

Chapter 7

75 ***Epigraph:*** Frederick Buechner, *Wishful Thinking: A Theological ABC* (New York: Harper & Row, 1973), 95.

76 ***J.C. Penney:*** I'm unable to trace this to an original source, but it is widely attributed to James Cash Penney. For instance, Peter Barron Stark, *The Only Leadership Book You'll Ever Need* (Newburyport, MA: Red Wheel/Weiser, 2009), 129.

78 ***Ford:*** I'm unable to trace this to an original source, but it is widely attributed to Henry Ford. For instance, Colin Shaw, *Revolutionize Your Customer Experience* (New York: Springer, 2004), 70.

79 ***Angelou:*** Colleen Curry, "Maya Angelou's Wisdom Distilled in 10 of Her Best Quotes," ABC News online, May 28, 2014, https://abcnews.go.com/Entertainment/maya-angelous-wisdom-distilled-10-best-quotes/story?id=23895284.

79 ***Barker:*** Joel A. Barker, website, accessed February 4, 2019, www.joelbarker.com.

Chapter 8

85 ***Epigraph:*** Quoted in Joe Griffith, *Speaker's Library of Business Stories, Anecdotes, and Humor* (New York: Barnes and Noble, 2000), 170.

86 ***the word* support:** *Merriam-Webster*, s.v. "support (*v.*)," accessed February 13, 2019, https://www.merriam-webster.com/dictionary/support.

87 ***Burkett:*** Larry Burkett, *The Complete Guide to Managing Your Money* (New York: BBS Publishing, 1996), 285.

89 ***Hawthorne:*** Nathaniel Hawthorne, *The Scarlet Letter* (New York: B&N Classics, 2003), 245.

Chapter 9

99 ***Epigraph:*** George Bernard Shaw, "Epistle Dedicatory to Arthur Bingham Walkley," *Man and Superman: A Comedy and a Philosophy* (1903), https://www.gutenberg.org/files/3328/3328-h/3328-h.htm.

Chapter 10

115 ***Epigraph:*** Quoted in Gil Bailie, *Violence Unveiled: Humanity at the Crossroads* (1996), xv.

119 ***Rokeach:*** James Kouzes and Barry Posner, *The Leadership Challenge Workbook Revised* (New York: Wiley, 2017), 35.

Chapter 11

123 ***Epigraph:*** Nehemiah 5:19 (NLT).

127 ***Chambers:*** Oswald Chambers, https://utmost.org/the-key-of-the-greater-work/.

Chapter 12

133 ***Epigraph:*** Attributed to first-century Roman philosopher Lucius Annaeus Seneca.

142 ***Schweitzer:*** Quoted in *Thoughts for Our Times*, ed. Erica Anderson, 1975, p. 51; accessed January 31, 2019, www.schweitzerfellowship.org/about/albert-schweitzer/philosophy/.

Chapter 13

145 ***Epigraph:*** From Stephen R. Lawhead, *Merlin*, The Pendragon Cycle, book 2 (New York: HarperCollins, 1988), 328.

146 ***Mr. Holland's Opus:*** Patrick Sheane Duncan (Writer) and Stephen Herek (Director). Mr. Holland's Opus [Motion picture]. United States: Buena Vista Pictures.

151 ***Steven Pressfield:*** Steven Pressfield, *The War of Art: Break through the Blocks and Win Your Inner Creative Battles*, paperback ed. (New York: Black Irish Entertainment, 2012), 40.

ACKNOWLEDGMENTS

It's really true what the apostle John said: "We love because He first loved us." Because I know where love originates, I'm most thankful to the Lord who loved me first. Nothing compares. It was God who placed in my life all of the people I'm about to mention. *Soli Deo gloria.*

As I reflect on the many people who have encouraged and helped me through the years, I'm overwhelmed by the depth and the number of kind, unselfish actions offered on my behalf. It is impossible for me to thank them all here, yet this book would not be possible without them.

I'll never forget first sharing about "leaving a legacy" with the leaders of a commercial construction company in upstate New York. Thank you, Phil McKinney. These conversations sparked a deep conviction within me that personal preparation could make a world of difference in impacting others. From there, the legacy course expanded to military installations, schools, churches, conference centers, and businesses.

A special thanks to my friend Len Woods, who provided his expertise in formatting the book's outline and then editing the first draft. Mike Vander Klipp, Todd Nigro, Eric Schmidt, Mike Echevarria, and Donna Pennell each made notable contributions early in this process.

I'd like to thank my agent Tim Beals of Credo Communications. Tim's vision for this book was inspiring.

It's been a great honor to work with Discovery House, and I'm especially grateful for the contributions of Miranda Gardner and Dawn Anderson. This book is better because of their expertise, passion, and hard work.

The people at Walk Thru the Bible have enriched my life for almost three decades and opened the door to a world of opportunity.

A significant influence in my life is Walt Wiley. Thank you, dear friend. Our years traveling together, working, and laughing at Winning with Encouragement (WWE) are among my most treasured memories.

To my friends at The Salvation Army, thank you for inviting me to teach in your wonderful community for almost twenty years. I'd especially like to thank Sarah and David Bentley, Nigel Cross, Judy Smith, Brian Jones,

Linda Manhardt, Tay Howard, Eda Hokum, Wayne and Cheryl Maynor, Jeff and Eloisa Martin, and Bill and Lisa Dickinson.

I've been blessed by friends who took a chance on me and opened doors of ministry throughout the United States and beyond. All of these adventures have shaped me. I'm thankful beyond words for Jim Walker, John and Debbie Houchens, Sid Stansell, Phil Tuttle, Ruth Westerholm, Bart Azzarelli, Barry Thompson, Brett DeYoung, Keith Moore, Jim Street, Bill Welte, Evan Benevides, Steve Keyes, Michael Wright, Bill Fischer, Kevin Moore, JB Collingsworth, John Warnock, Keith Allen, Dan Roberts, Jan Kary, Steve Roach, CA Phillips, Mike Sorrow, David Warda, and Ronny Jones. This list could go on and on.

Our small group at church sharpens us every time we meet. Without my permission and despite my protest, the group named us "HodgePodge." I've learned to just give in to Mike and Lani, Darryl and Janet, Donnie and Jeanette, Brian and Seema, and Tony and Pam. Our journey with them has been extraordinary.

My wife's family has had a profound impact on me. Linda and Chuck, thank you for raising such a beautiful and loving family. Cindy, Missy and Mark, Jane and Donnie, Nelson and Laura, your support through the years means the world to me.

My mom and dad were the finest people I've ever known. Thankfully I shared that with them a few years before they passed away. My dear brother Kevin passed away as well, leaving a hole in my life for sure. There's hardly a day that passes that I don't think of my mom or dad or Kevin and praise God for their influence.

My brother Dan (and his wife Judy) and my sister Robin (and her husband Jim) have been a constant source of guidance for me, beginning with my first memories. Their impact on my life cannot be overstated.

It's not possible for any dad to be prouder of his children than I am. Elizabeth, Jameson, and Spencer, it's impossible to express how happy and fulfilled each of you make me.

My final acknowledgment is for my wife and primary partner in ministry. Pam, looking back on those moments when we first got to know each other, I often think of Elizabeth Barrett Browning's words: "The face of all the world is changed, I think, since first I heard the footsteps of thy soul." Indeed, my life did change. What I was unprepared for was how much better it would be. Every day with you is a gift undeserved. You are my dearest friend, the one who makes me laugh the most, and my greatest champion. You are treasured, my love.

Enjoy this book? Help us get the word out!

Share a link to the book or
mention it on social media

Write a review on your blog, on a retailer site,
or on our website (dhp.org)

Pick up another copy to share with someone

Recommend this book for your
church, book club, or small group

Follow Discovery House on
social media and join the discussion

Contact us to share your thoughts:

 @discoveryhouse

 @DiscoveryHouse

Discovery House
P.O. Box 3566
Grand Rapids, MI 49501 USA

Phone: 1-800-653-8333
Email: books@dhp.org
Web: dhp.org